Yem S. Fong
Suzanne M. Ward
Editors

The Changing Landscape for Electronic Resources: Content, Access, Delivery, and Legal Issues

The Changing Landscape for Electronic Resources: Content, Access, Delivery, and Legal Issues has been co-published simultaneously as *Journal of Library Administration*, Volume 40, Numbers 1/2 2004.

The Haworth Information Press
An Imprint of The Haworth Press, Inc.

The Changing Landscape for Electronic Resources: Content, Access, Delivery, and Legal Issues

The Changing Landscape for Electronic Resources: Content, Access, Delivery, and Legal Issues has been co-published simultaneously as *Journal of Library Administration*, Volume 40, Numbers 1/2 2004.

The *Journal of Library Administration* Monographic "Separates"

The Changing Landscape for Electronic Resources: Content, Access, Delivery, and Legal Issues, edited by Yem S. Fong, MLS, and Suzanne M. Ward, MA (Vol. 40, No. 1/2, 2004). *Focuses on various aspects of electronic resources for libraries, including statewide resource-sharing initiatives, licensing issues, open source software, standards, and scholarly publishing.*

Improved Access to Information: Portals, Content Selection, and Digital Information, edited by Sul H. Lee (Vol. 39, No. 4, 2003). *Examines how improved electronic resources can allow libraries to provide an increasing amount of digital information to an ever-expanding patron base.*

Digital Images and Art Libraries in the Twenty-First Century, edited by Susan Wyngaard, MLS (Vol. 39, No. 2/3, 2003). *Provides an in-depth look at the technology that art librarians must understand in order to work effectively in today's digital environment.*

The Twenty-First Century Art Librarian, edited by Terrie L. Wilson, MLS (Vol. 39, No. 1, 2003). *"A MUST-READ addition to every art, architecture, museum, and visual resources library bookshelf." (Betty Jo Irvine, PhD, Fine Arts Librarian, Indiana University)*

The Strategic Stewardship of Cultural Resources: To Preserve and Protect, edited by Andrea T. Merrill, BA (Vol. 38, No. 1/2/3/4, 2003). *Leading library, museum, and archival professionals share their expertise on a wide variety of preservation and security issues.*

Distance Learning Library Services: The Tenth Off-Campus Library Services Conference, edited by Patrick B. Mahoney (Vol. 37, No. 1/2/3/4, 2002). *Explores the pitfalls of providing information services to distance students and suggests ways to avoid them.*

Electronic Resources and Collection Development, edited by Sul H. Lee (Vol. 36, No. 3, 2002). *Shows how electronic resources have impacted traditional collection development policies and practices.*

Information Literacy Programs: Successes and Challenges, edited by Patricia Durisin, MLIS (Vol. 36, No. 1/2, 2002). *Examines Web-based collaboration, teamwork with academic and administrative colleagues, evidence-based librarianship, and active learning strategies in library instruction programs.*

Evaluating the Twenty-First Century Library: The Association of Research Libraries New Measures Initiative, 1997-2001, edited by Donald L. DeWitt, PhD (Vol. 35, No. 4, 2001). *This collection of articles (thirteen of which previously appeared in ARL's bimonthly newsletter/report on research issues and actions) examines the Association of Research Libraries' "new measures" initiative.*

Impact of Digital Technology on Library Collections and Resource Sharing, edited by Sul H. Lee (Vol. 35, No. 3, 2001). *Shows how digital resources have changed the traditional academic library.*

Libraries and Electronic Resources: New Partnerships, New Practices, New Perspectives, edited by Pamela L. Higgins (Vol. 35, No. 1/2, 2001). *An essential guide to the Internet's impact on electronic resources management past, present, and future.*

Diversity Now: People, Collections, and Services in Academic Libraries, edited by Teresa Y. Neely, PhD, and Kuang-Hwei (Janet) Lee-Smeltzer, MS, MSLIS (Vol. 33, No. 1/2/3/4, 2001). *Examines multicultural trends in academic libraries' staff and users, types of collections, and services offered.*

Leadership in the Library and Information Science Professions: Theory and Practice, edited by Mark D. Winston, MLS, PhD (Vol. 32, No. 3/4, 2001). *Offers fresh ideas for developing and using leadership skills, including recruiting potential leaders, staff training and development, issues of gender and ethnic diversity, and budget strategies for success.*

Off-Campus Library Services, edited by Ann Marie Casey (Vol. 31, No. 3/4, 2001 and Vol. 32, No. 1/2, 2001). *This informative volume examines various aspects of off-campus, or distance learning. It explores training issues for library staff, Web site development, changing roles for librarians, the uses of conferencing software, library support for Web-based courses, library agreements and how to successfully negotiate them, and much more!*

Research Collections and Digital Information, edited by Sul H. Lee (Vol. 31, No. 2, 2000). *Offers new strategies for collecting, organizing, and accessing library materials in the digital age.*

Academic Research on the Internet: Options for Scholars & Libraries, edited by Helen Laurence, MLS, EdD, and William Miller, MLS, PhD (Vol. 30, No. 1/2/3/4, 2000). *"Emphasizes quality over quantity. . . . Presents the reader with the best research-oriented Web sites in the field. A state-of-the-art review of academic use of the Internet as well as a guide to the best Internet sites and services. . . . A useful addition for any academic library." (David A. Tyckoson, MLS, Head of Reference, California State University, Fresno)*

Management for Research Libraries Cooperation, edited by Sul H. Lee (Vol. 29, No. 3/4, 2000). *Delivers sound advice, models, and strategies for increasing sharing between institutions to maximize the amount of printed and electronic research material you can make available in your library while keeping costs under control.*

Integration in the Library Organization, edited by Christine E. Thompson, PhD (Vol. 29, No. 2, 1999). *Provides librarians with the necessary tools to help libraries balance and integrate public and technical services and to improve the capability of libraries to offer patrons quality services and large amounts of information.*

Library Training for Staff and Customers, edited by Sara Ramser Beck, MLS, MBA (Vol. 29, No. 1, 1999). *This comprehensive book is designed to assist library professionals involved in presenting or planning training for library staff members and customers. You will explore ideas for effective general reference training, training on automated systems, training in specialized subjects such as African American history and biography, and training for areas such as patents and trademarks, and business subjects.* Library Training for Staff and Customers *answers numerous training questions and is an excellent guide for planning staff development.*

Collection Development in the Electronic Environment: Shifting Priorities, edited by Sul H. Lee (Vol. 28, No. 4, 1999). *Through case studies and firsthand experiences, this volume discusses meeting the needs of scholars at universities, budgeting issues, user education, staffing in the electronic age, collaborating libraries and resources, and how vendors meet the needs of different customers.*

The Age Demographics of Academic Librarians: A Profession Apart, by Stanley J. Wilder (Vol. 28, No. 3, 1999). *The average age of librarians has been increasing dramatically since 1990. This unique book will provide insights on how this demographic issue can impact a library and what can be done to make the effects positive.*

Collection Development in a Digital Environment, edited by Sul H. Lee (Vol. 28, No. 1, 1999). *Explores ethical and technological dilemmas of collection development and gives several suggestions on how a library can successfully deal with these challenges and provide patrons with the information they need.*

Scholarship, Research Libraries, and Global Publishing, by Jutta Reed-Scott (Vol. 27, No. 3/4, 1999). *This book documents a research project in conjunction with the Association of Research Libraries (ARL) that explores the issue of foreign acquisition and how it affects collection in international studies, area studies, collection development, and practices of international research libraries.*

Managing Multicultural Diversity in the Library: Principles and Issues for Administrators, edited by Mark Winston (Vol. 27, No. 1/2, 1999). *Defines diversity, clarifies why it is important to address issues of diversity, and identifies goals related to diversity and how to go about achieving those goals.*

Information Technology Planning, edited by Lori A. Goetsch (Vol. 26, No. 3/4, 1999). *Offers innovative approaches and strategies useful in your library and provides some food for thought about information technology as we approach the millennium.*

The Economics of Information in the Networked Environment, edited by Meredith A. Butler, MLS, and Bruce R. Kingma, PhD (Vol. 26, No. 1/2, 1998). *"A book that should be read both by information professionals and by administrators, faculty and others who share a collective concern to provide the most information to the greatest number at the lowest cost in the networked environment." (Thomas J. Galvin, PhD, Professor of Information Science and Policy, University at Albany, State University of New York)*

OCLC 1967-1997: Thirty Years of Furthering Access to the World's Information, edited by K. Wayne Smith (Vol. 25, No. 2/3/4, 1998). *"A rich–and poignantly personal, at times–historical account of what is surely one of this century's most important developments in librarianship." (Deanna B. Marcum, PhD, President, Council on Library and Information Resources, Washington, DC)*

Management of Library and Archival Security: From the Outside Looking In, edited by Robert K. O'Neill, PhD (Vol. 25, No. 1, 1998). *"Provides useful advice and on-target insights for professionals caring for valuable documents and artifacts." (Menzi L. Behrnd-Klodt, JD, Attorney/Archivist, Klodt and Associates, Madison, WI)*

Economics of Digital Information: Collection, Storage, and Delivery, edited by Sul H. Lee (Vol. 24, No. 4, 1997). *Highlights key concepts and issues vital to a library's successful venture into the digital environment and helps you understand why the transition from the printed page to the digital packet has been problematic for both creators of proprietary materials and users of those materials.*

The Academic Library Director: Reflections on a Position in Transition, edited by Frank D'Andraia, MLS (Vol. 24, No. 3, 1997). *"A useful collection to have whether you are seeking a position as director or conducting a search for one." (College & Research Libraries News)*

Emerging Patterns of Collection Development in Expanding Resource Sharing, Electronic Information, and Network Environment, edited by Sul H. Lee (Vol. 24, No. 1/2, 1997). *"The issues it deals with are common to us all. We all need to make our funds go further and our resources work harder, and there are ideas here which we can all develop." (The Library Association Record)*

Interlibrary Loan/Document Delivery and Customer Satisfaction: Strategies for Redesigning Services, edited by Pat L. Weaver-Meyers, Wilbur A. Stolt, and Yem S. Fong (Vol. 23, No. 1/2, 1997). *"No interlibrary loan department supervisor at any mid-sized to large college or university library can afford not to read this book." (Gregg Sapp, MLS, MEd, Head of Access Services, University of Miami, Richter Library, Coral Gables, Florida)*

Access, Resource Sharing and Collection Development, edited by Sul H. Lee (Vol. 22, No. 4, 1996). *Features continuing investigation and discussion of important library issues, specifically the role of libraries in acquiring, storing, and disseminating information in different formats.*

Managing Change in Academic Libraries, edited by Joseph J. Branin (Vol. 22, No. 2/3, 1996). *"Touches on several aspects of academic library management, emphasizing the changes that are occurring at the present time. . . . Recommended this title for individuals or libraries interested in management aspects of academic libraries." (RQ American Library Association)*

Libraries and Student Assistants: Critical Links, edited by William K. Black, MLS (Vol. 21, No. 3/4, 1995). *"A handy reference work on many important aspects of managing student assistants. . . . Solid, useful information on basic management issues in this work and several chapters are useful for experienced managers." (The Journal of Academic Librarianship)*

The Future of Resource Sharing, edited by Shirley K. Baker and Mary E. Jackson, MLS (Vol. 21, No. 1/2, 1995). *"Recommended for library and information science schools because of its balanced presentation of the ILL/document delivery issues." (Library Acquisitions: Practice and Theory)*

The Future of Information Services, edited by Virginia Steel, MA, and C. Brigid Welch, MLS (Vol. 20, No. 3/4, 1995). *"The leadership discussions will be useful for library managers as will the discussions of how library structures and services might work in the next century." (Australian Special Libraries)*

Monographic "Separates" list continued at the back

The Changing Landscape for Electronic Resources: Content, Access, Delivery, and Legal Issues

Yem S. Fong
Suzanne M. Ward
Editors

The Changing Landscape for Electronic Resources: Content, Access, Delivery, and Legal Issues has been co-published simultaneously as *Journal of Library Administration*, Volume 40, Numbers 1/2 2004.

The Haworth Information Press®
An Imprint of The Haworth Press, Inc.

New York • London • Victoria (AU)
www.HaworthPress.com

Published by

The Haworth Information Press®, 10 Alice Street, Binghamton, NY 13904-1580 USA

The Haworth Information Press® is an imprint of The Haworth Press, Inc., 10 Alice Street, Binghamton, NY 13904-1580 USA.

The Changing Landscape for Electronic Resources: Content, Access, Delivery, and Legal Issues has been co-published simultaneously as *Journal of Library Administration*™, Volume 40, Numbers 1/2 2004.

The development, preparation, and publication of this work has been undertaken with great care. However, the publisher, employees, editors, and agents of The Haworth Press and all imprints of The Haworth Press, Inc., including The Haworth Medical Press® and Pharmaceutical Products Press®, are not responsible for any errors contained herein or for consequences that may ensue from use of materials or information contained in this work. Opinions expressed by the author(s) are not necessarily those of The Haworth Press, Inc. With regard to case studies, identities and circumstances of individuals discussed herein have been changed to protect confidentiality. Any resemblance to actual persons, living or dead, is entirely coincidental.

Cover design by Jennifer M. Gaska.

Library of Congress Cataloging-in-Publication Data

The changing landscape for electronic resources : content, access, delivery, and legal issues / Yem S. Fong, Suzanne M. Ward, editors.
　　　p. cm.
　　　"Co-published simultaneously as Journal of Library Administration, volume 40, numbers 1/2 2004."
　　　Includes bibliographical references and index.
　　　ISBN 0-7890-2440-3 (alk. paper) – ISBN 0-7890-2441-1 (soft cover : alk. paper)
　　　1. Digital libraries. 2. Libraries–Special collections–Electronic information resources. 3. Library cooperation. 4. Interlibrary loans. 5. Scholarly publishing. 6. Open source software. I. Fong, Yem S. II. Ward, Suzanne M. III. Journal of library administration.
ZA4080 .C47 2004
025'.00285–dc22
　　　　　　　　　　　　　　　　　　　　　　　　　　　　　　　　　　　2004009974

Indexing, Abstracting & Website/Internet Coverage

Journal of Library Administration

This section provides you with a list of major indexing & abstracting services. That is to say, each service began covering this periodical during the year noted in the right column. Most Websites which are listed below have indicated that they will either post, disseminate, compile, archive, cite or alert their own Website users with research-based content from this work. (This list is as current as the copyright date of this publication.)

Abstracting, Website/Indexing Coverage . . . . Year When Coverage Began

- *AATA Online: Abstracts of International Conservation Literature*
  (formerly Art & Archeology Technical Abstracts)
  <http://aata.getty.edu>. **2004**

- *Academic Abstracts/CD-ROM* **1993**

- *Academic Search: database of 2,000 selected academic serials,*
  updated monthly: EBSCO Publishing **1995**

- *Academic Search Elite (EBSCO)* **1993**

- *AGRICOLA Database <http://www.natl.usda.gov/ag98>* **1991**

- *Business & Company ProFile ASAP on CD-ROM*
  <http://www.galegroup.com> **1996**

- *Business ASAP* **1993**

- *Business ASAP–International <http://www.galegroup.com>* **1984**

- *Business International and Company ProFile ASAP*
  <http://www.galegroup.com> **1996**

- *CNPIEC Reference Guide: Chinese National Directory*
  of Foreign Periodicals **1995**

- *Computer and Information Systems Abstracts*
  <http://www.csa.com>. **2004**

- *Current Articles on Library Literature and Services (CALLS)* **1992**

- *Current Cites [Digital Libraries] [Electronic Publishing]*
  [Multimedia & Hypermedia] [Networks & Networking]
  [General] **2000**

(continued)

(continued)

*Exact start date to come.

(continued)

Special Bibliographic Notes related to special journal issues (separates) and indexing/abstracting:

- indexing/abstracting services in this list will also cover material in any "separate" that is co-published simultaneously with Haworth's special thematic journal issue or DocuSerial. Indexing/abstracting usually covers material at the article/chapter level.
- monographic co-editions are intended for either non-subscribers or libraries which intend to purchase a second copy for their circulating collections.
- monographic co-editions are reported to all jobbers/wholesalers/approval plans. The source journal is listed as the "series" to assist the prevention of duplicate purchasing in the same manner utilized for books-in-series.
- to facilitate user/access services all indexing/abstracting services are encouraged to utilize the co-indexing entry note indicated at the bottom of the first page of each article/chapter/contribution.
- this is intended to assist a library user of any reference tool (whether print, electronic, online, or CD-ROM) to locate the monographic version if the library has purchased this version but not a subscription to the source journal.
- individual articles/chapters in any Haworth publication are also available through the Haworth Document Delivery Service (HDDS).

The Changing Landscape for Electronic Resources: Content, Access, Delivery, and Legal Issues

CONTENTS

ABOUT THE EDITORS

Yem S. Fong, MLS, is an Associate Professor and Faculty Director, Electronic Resources Development and Information Delivery at the University of Colorado Libraries, Boulder. She has been engaged in library management and resource sharing for over twenty years, and is the author of numerous articles on interlibrary loan, fee-based services, and Asian American women's studies. She is active in state and national committees, including the Greater Western Library Alliance, ACRL FISC-L Discussion Group and the Colorado Interlibrary Loan Committee. She is a graduate of the University of Colorado, University of California, Berkeley, and the Japan America Institute of Management.

Suzanne M. Ward, AMLS, MA, is Head of Access Services at the Purdue University Libraries in West Lafayette, Indiana. She has written extensively about managing library fee-based information services and about library resource sharing issues in publications such as *Advances in Library Resource Sharing, The Reference Librarian, The Acquisitions Librarian, Journal of Access Services*, and *Journal of Interlibrary Loan, Document Delivery & Information Supply*. She holds degrees from UCLA, the University of Michigan, and Memphis State University.

Introduction

In the changing information landscape, electronic content has an un-
deniable impact on how libraries provide access to library resources. As
publishers offer greater incentives and consortial discounts for databases, e-journals, and e-books, the move to "electronic only" has significant ramifications for traditional library services. The fallout from these
changes is that libraries must reposition their roles not only physically,
but also remotely and electronically through the Internet and distributed
networks.

This collection of articles considers the effects and challenges of
electronic content on resource sharing. To highlight the complexities of
the electronic environment for resource sharing, the editors have included articles on copyright and licensing, open source software, international data standards, and scholarly publishing.

Brenda Bailey-Hainer, Director, Networking and Resource Sharing
at the Colorado State Library, offers insights into the challenges of implementing a statewide electronic interlibrary loan request system
among multi-type and multi-size libraries with widely divergent technology and expertise. She describes the lessons learned, and the potential savings for libraries that moved to this standards-driven statewide
electronic system.

Donna Ferullo, Director, University Copyright Office at the Purdue
University Libraries, considers the major issues involved with copyright and licensing for academic libraries in the digital environment.

[Haworth co-indexing entry note]: "Introduction." Fong, Yem S., and Suzanne M. Ward. Co-published
simultaneously in *Journal of Library Administration* (The Haworth Information Press, an imprint of The
Haworth Press, Inc.) Vol. 40, No. 1/2, 2004, pp. 1-3; and: *The Changing Landscape for Electronic Resources: Content, Access, Delivery, and Legal Issues* (ed: Yem S. Fong, and Suzanne M. Ward) The Haworth
Information Press, an imprint of The Haworth Press, Inc., 2004, pp. 1-3. Single or multiple copies of this article are available for a fee from The Haworth Document Delivery Service [1-800-HAWORTH, 9:00 a.m. -
5:00 p.m. (EST). E-mail address: docdelivery@haworthpress.com].

Digital Object Identifier: 10.1300/J111v40n01_01

She discusses the interpretation of copyright laws in the area of e-re-serves, licensing, document delivery, and fair use. Continuing on this theme, Kathleen Smalldon, Associate University Librarian, Northern Arizona University, and Jeffrey Carrico, Acquisitions Librarian, North-ern Arizona University, offer a model for negotiating with e-content publishers for the right to provide interlibrary loan delivery from and in electronic formats to borrowing partners. They describe a partnership between interlibrary loan and collection development in working with licenses and publishers.

For electronic resource systems to operate efficiently, technology, Internet applications, protocols, and standards all play important and in-terconnected roles. As Jeff Steely, Assistant Director for Client Ser-vices, Baylor University, notes, open source software offers many options to libraries willing to invest in developing and enhancing soft-ware products that are freely offered on the Web. Steely looks at open source software applications specifically targeted to interlibrary loan functionality.

Robert McDonald, Assistant Director of Libraries for Technology, Media Services and Digital Libraries, Florida State University, and Catherine Jannik, Digital Initiatives Manager, Library and Informa-tion Center, Georgia Institute of Technology, take open source one step further and examine the issues surrounding implementation of the MyLibrary open source portal at Auburn University. They consider the broader access picture in looking at how a portal can provide a user centered approach to multi-database searching and access to e-con-tent.

Julie Blume Nye, Senior Product Designer, Fretwell-Downing, Inc., considers the progress in developing core standards, protocols, and data elements in resource sharing functionality. She explains how standards, such as Z39.50, are essential to the infrastructure for search and re-trieval, messaging, and sharing information across vendor platforms for online catalogs, interlibrary loan systems and other applications.

Thomas Bacher, Director, Purdue University Press, takes a long-range view of scholarly digitization and distribution and in particular looks at the academic publishing model. He ponders how universities as publishers will survive and compete in the current electronic publishing marketplace. He also discusses how academia can support scholarly re-search in ways that are affordable and attainable, while promoting the retention of authors' rights for copyright and distribution.

While these articles discuss the challenges and potential pitfalls of managing electronic content in the evolving modern library, the authors also anticipate a future in which electronic access improves the range, speed, quality, and quantity of cost-effective information services for a library's own patrons as well as for its resource sharing partners.

Yem S. Fong
Suzanne M. Ward

Multi-Type Statewide Resource Sharing: The Colorado SWIFT Experience

Brenda K. Bailey-Hainer

SUMMARY. Colorado is one of a number of states that have implemented a locally hosted statewide, Web-based interlibrary loan system. The initial target audience was small- to medium-sized libraries of any type that had not previously automated their interlibrary loan processes. After a year and a half of operation, staff from 275 public, academic, school, and special libraries have been trained on SWIFT (StateWide ILL Fast Track), and current transactions are about 103,000 annually. A cost analysis showed that libraries using the system have reduced their costs for both borrowing and lending. *[Article copies available for a fee from The Haworth Document Delivery Service: 1-800-HAWORTH. E-mail address: <docdelivery@haworthpress. com> Website: <http://www.HaworthPress.com> © 2004 by The Haworth Press, Inc. All rights reserved.]*

KEYWORDS. Resource sharing, interlibrary loan, statewide initiatives, multi-type, patron-initiated

INTRODUCTION

Many state library agencies have created virtual one stop searching options to locate resources scattered throughout their state's public, aca-

Brenda K. Bailey-Hainer is Director, Networking and Resource Sharing, Colorado State Library (E-mail: bailey_b@cde.state.co.us).

[Haworth co-indexing entry note]: "Multi-Type Statewide Resource Sharing: The Colorado SWIFT Experience." Bailey-Hainer, Brenda K. Co-published simultaneously in *Journal of Library Administration* (The Haworth Information Press, an imprint of The Haworth Press, Inc.) Vol. 40, No. 1/2, 2004, pp. 5-22; and: *The Changing Landscape for Electronic Resources: Content, Access, Delivery, and Legal Issues* (ed: Yem S. Fong, and Suzanne M. Ward) The Haworth Information Press, an imprint of The Haworth Press, Inc., 2004, pp. 5-22. Single or multiple copies of this article are available for a fee from The Haworth Document Delivery Service [1-800-HAWORTH, 9:00 a.m. - 5:00 p.m. (EST). E-mail address: docdelivery@haworthpress.com].

Digital Object Identifier: 10.1300/J111v40n01_02

demic, school, and special libraries. These projects are often the result of a combination of state library missions and federal funding priorities. The primary federal funding program for state library projects, LSTA (Library Services and Technology Act), outlines two broad priorities that relate to resource sharing. The first focuses on "using technology for information sharing between libraries and between libraries and other community services." The second is for programs that "make library resources more accessible to urban, rural, or low-income residents, and others who have difficulty using library services" (Institute of Museum and Library Services, 2003).

While identifying the existence of needed materials in a state is a fine beginning, the crucial next step is to obtain the material once it has been located. Statewide interlibrary loan (ILL) systems bridge the gap between identifying useful materials and delivering those materials to the user's home library by handling the electronic request routing piece of the puzzle. In addition to responding to the priorities outlined in LSTA, many states are motivated to provide such networks to significantly reduce the cost of intra-state interlibrary loan, especially for small, often rural libraries. Colorado is just one of an increasing number of states using LSTA funds to create its own statewide interlibrary loan networks to facilitate the electronic requesting and tracking of materials. This article provides information on different resource sharing models, some examples of implemented models, and an overview of the Colorado project, specifically including lessons learned throughout the project.

STATEWIDE RESOURCE SHARING MODELS

Many more options exist today for state library agencies interested in implementing locally hosted resource sharing initiatives than there were a decade ago. The first of these includes creating a physical union catalog, either on CD-ROM or online, and using it as the location source for materials to be borrowed. The vendor that creates the union catalog, or a different vendor, supplies the interlibrary loan software to route the requests to potential lenders and track requests throughout their life cycle.

A second model is a variation on the first one, and uses a Z39.50 client to create a virtual union catalog through distributed multi-cast searching of individual library catalogs in the state. Again, interlibrary loan software may be provided either by the vendor that provides the Z39.50 client, or through a second vendor.

A third model addresses cases where it is not practical, due to costs or technological barriers, to create either a single physical union catalog or to connect separately to each individual library catalog in the state. This model involves creating a hybrid of the two models mentioned above. Large libraries' catalogs may be accessed using a Z39.50 client, and the remainder of the library catalogs may be aggregated into one or more physical union catalogs that are accessed via Z39.50, together creating a single virtual statewide resource.

Another potential model that is not yet in production involves using OCLC's WorldCat as the de facto union catalog. This model requires that most of the libraries in the state catalog their materials using OCLC, or that the state library agency or regional library systems cover the cost of uploading their member libraries' holdings into WorldCat. The holdings of other significant collections may be accessed along with the scoped WorldCat holdings by using Z39.50, creating yet another variation of the virtual union catalog.

Single-type consortia have enjoyed significant success using a single integrated local system to create a physical union catalog. One of the best-known examples of this model is OhioLINK (Ohio Library and Information Network), a large consortia of academic libraries, which uses the Innovative Interfaces INN-Reach system. For large multi-type networks that include a mixture of public, academic, school, and special libraries, however, it is highly unlikely that a single brand of integrated local system will suffice for all library types involved.

In reality, states are using a variety of the methods described above. According to the National Center for Education Statistics (NCES), which collects data from state library agencies, the trend over the last four years is that the number of state library agencies running Z39.50 gateways has declined slightly from twenty-one to twenty. The number of state library agencies creating Web-based union catalogs has remained level at thirty, and those with CD-ROM union catalogs have decreased from eighteen to twelve (see Figure 1) (Kroe, 2001; U.S. Department of Education, 1999, 2000 and 2002).

The WISCAT solution used in Wisconsin, which is a physical union catalog combined with an interlibrary loan module from a second vendor, is an example of the first model of statewide resource sharing mentioned above. A veteran of statewide resource sharing, Wisconsin began in 1983 with a microfiche catalog, and moved to CD-ROM in the late 1980s. In 1997, WISCAT was made available over the Internet with a physical union catalog product by Brodart, and a module developed for them called QuILL. The QuILL program allowed libraries to create ILL

FIGURE 1. State Library Agency Union Catalog Solutions, 1998-2001

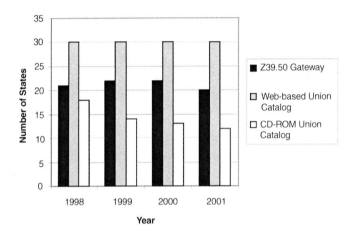

requests and route them to other libraries, and the program managed the telecommunications and record-keeping processes for participating libraries. QuILL was not widely distributed or marketed by Brodart, and in 2002, the Wisconsin Division for Libraries and Community Learning sought a different solution. Still based on the physical union catalog model, Wisconsin moved to Auto-Graphics to create and support it. The union catalog now contains the holdings of approximately 1,200 libraries, including the records of the University of Wisconsin system (Drew, 2003).

Wisconsin then contracted with Fretwell-Downing (FDI), Inc., for the Virtual Document Exchange software (VDX). The VDX software is hosted and run for Wisconsin by FDI in Kansas City, Missouri, using an ASP (applications service provider) model. Currently there are about five hundred libraries use ILL through the system, and the monthly volume averages 27,000 transactions. Wisconsin also has continued a practice from its Brodart days of sharing resources with Minnesota. MINITEX, a publicly supported network of libraries based in Minneapolis that serves a three-state region, has a location code and password on the WISCAT system. Since Minnesota recently also licensed the FDI VDX software, the two states expect to share resources directly using international standards protocols and data messaging (ISO ILL 10160/10161) to link directly between the two VDX systems (Drew, 2003).

The state of New Jersey implemented its first statewide resource sharing system in 1999, described earlier in the second model of statewide systems. Multi-type libraries throughout the state used the epixtech Resource Sharing System (RSS), which relied on a distributed Z39.50 virtual union catalog approach. While it did support resource sharing, the system had two drawbacks that kept it from functioning well in the statewide environment. First, a Web interface for the system was not available, a feature that was desirable for a large multi-type initiative with many small participating libraries. Secondly, RSS required that specific software be loaded on individual workstations at libraries participating in the project. State library staff found it frustrating and labor intensive to drive around the state upgrading workstations at individual libraries whenever new software versions and patches were released (Schatz, 2003).

In 2002, New Jersey signed a contract with Auto-Graphics, Inc. to create JerseyCat, a solution that now adheres to model three. This service makes it easier for small libraries to participate as well as large ones. While the system supports the Z39.50 connections to the collections of larger libraries, Auto-Graphics is also building a physical union catalog of selected libraries for JerseyCat. Any library with fewer than 100,000 holdings, or which does not support Z39.50 searching, may contribute their holdings to the union catalog. Smaller libraries also may participate in the program by being part of a regional consortium and aggregating their holdings there, which can be accessed via Z39.50. The system is still ramping up, but over five hundred libraries have already signed participation agreements. Most public libraries are involved already, and the New Jersey State Library is actively recruiting additional academic and school libraries to participate (Schatz, 2003).

Many other statewide initiatives are using different vendor variations on the three models. Access Pennsylvania has been testing an Innovative Interfaces union catalog coupled with Fretwell-Downing VDX to move ILL requests around. OPLIN (Ohio Public Library Information Network) is using Fretwell-Downing VDX combined with FDI's ZPORTAL product to create the virtual union catalog and to support interlibrary loan. Similar to New Jersey, Kansas employs a single Auto-Graphics solution for both physical union catalog and ILL system. Illinois is currently piloting a proposed solution from OCLC Inc., that uses the WorldCat catalog as the basis for scoping down to show just the state's holdings. A combination of the OCLC ILL Service and Direct Request functionality is then used to fulfill any requests placed by either library staff or users. Wyoming recently converted from a statewide DRA system to a Sirsi system, and is implementing Fretwell-Downing VDX for interlibrary loan.

These are just some of the examples of statewide resource sharing projects that are being implemented using the three models described above.

THE COLORADO EXPERIENCE–SWIFT

In 2000, Colorado was in a position similar to that of other states. Colorado has a long-standing history of multi-type library cooperation and resource sharing. To build on an already strong resource sharing program, Colorado State Library staff had implemented a Z39.50 gateway to library catalogs throughout the state using OCLC's SiteSearch WebZ software (now available as open source). The State Library had been interested in creating a statewide interlibrary loan system as early as 1997, and had contracted with an outside consultant to review patron-initiated interlibrary loan software and create general requirements. At the time the study was completed, the consultant concluded that there was no software package on the market that could do what Colorado libraries wanted (Fong, 1997).

By the time the State Library appointed a new Director of Networking and Resource Sharing in 1999, the situation had changed. A number of vendors had software products on the market that were designed specifically for large consortia. The State Library convened a committee of eighteen people representing all types of libraries. The committee updated the consultant's original requirements document and issued it as an RFI in spring 2000. After reviewing responses and demonstrations from four vendors, the group concluded that Fretwell-Downing's VDX software was the best choice for Colorado.

VDX was a good fit for several reasons. The software is independent of any integrated local system platform, so participants can join without being forced to migrate to a specific local system. In addition, Colorado already had created a virtual union catalog–the Colorado Virtual Library–based on the Z39.50 standard. VDX also relies on Z39.50 to search library catalogs to search for potential lenders of materials, and there was no requirement to build a physical union catalog. The existing Colorado virtual union catalog meant that the Z39.50 infrastructure was already in place. Running an interlibrary loan system locally requires local technical expertise and support; Colorado already had the staff available who were used to supporting the virtual union catalog.

Another reason that the distributed model was highly desirable in Colorado is that many libraries do not use OCLC for cataloging. An estimated 1.5 million holdings in the state are not on OCLC, and are available primarily through direct local system access or through Z39.50 connections to the catalogs.

The initial costs of implementing the service were funded through a LSTA grant of $225,435 received in summer 2000. This funding covered the initial software license, training of operations staff, creation and printing of documentation for end user training, and expenses for training library staff throughout the state. Twenty-nine libraries participated in a pilot during the first year of operation while the service was gradually rolled out to other institutions.

Officially released in September 2001, the system–named SWIFT (StateWide ILL Fast Track)–continues to utilize SiteSearch WebZ for the portal/front end searching mechanism for public use. Fretwell-Downing VDX has been integrated with it for purposes of patron-initiated requesting. The staff searching interface utilizes Fretwell-Downing's ZPORTAL software.

At the end of the first year and a half of operation, SWIFT staff trained and profiled about 275 school, public, academic, institutional, and special libraries. Of these, 203 actively used the system during the last six months: 108 public libraries, forty-nine school media centers, twenty-three academic libraries, fourteen correctional facilities, five regional library system offices, and four special libraries. Figure 2 shows the distribution by institutional type.

A workflow analysis comparing the costs and time libraries spent on ILL before and after implementing SWIFT was part of the evaluation requirement for the LSTA grant. Participants undertook this study in spring 2001. Of the original twenty-nine pilot libraries, twenty-three responded to the request to fill out workflow work form charts. Libraries were asked to provide specific benchmarking data, for both before and after SWIFT was implemented at their institution. Components of the work form included various ILL staff members' salaries to identify staff time and costs; automation and courier costs; the number of steps in their borrowing and lending processes; and what each step required as far as manual or automated processing. All of the information that follows related to workflow and cost analysis is taken from this study (Madsen, 2001).

Staffing costs were calculated down to the minute. The total number of minutes of each request times the staff cost per minute provided staffing cost data. Courier costs per day were divided by the number of requests received and sent each day. The minutes per request times the automation costs per minute were added to the sum of the staffing and courier costs to provide the summary data.

FIGURE 2. SWIFT Membership by Library Type

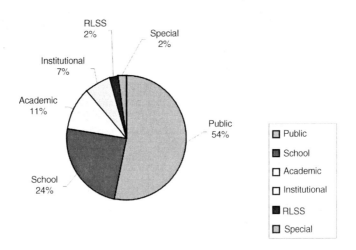

The results of the study showed that small-and medium-sized libraries, many of which previously used typed ALA forms and faxes, saved
money by using SWIFT for borrowing (see Figure 3). Most of these
same libraries saw a decrease in the costs for lending materials as well
(see Figure 4).

Libraries also saw a reduction in the time needed to complete requests.
Figure 5 shows the number of minutes taken by small public libraries to
complete a request.

One of the project's primary goals was to automate the requesting process for small and medium libraries and to reduce their costs. Another important aspect concerned large libraries as lenders. Since their collections
are invaluable for statewide resource sharing initiatives, it was critical
that they also realize benefits from the project. The workflow analysis
showed that there was also a reduction in the cost of lending by large public libraries using SWIFT (see Figure 6). Some of this cost reduction may
have been due to the fact that these libraries were able to use an automated
process for lending to small libraries rather than dealing with ALA forms
and faxes.

The cost analysis shown in the figures includes only the costs in-
curred at the individual library for lending or borrowing. The LSTA
grant covered the initial cost of implementing the project. The Colorado
State Library provides SWIFT to all libraries in the state at no charge to
them; the state library also absorbs on-going costs. These costs include

FIGURE 3. Costs for Borrowing Returnables, Small Public Libraries, Before and After Implementing SWIFT

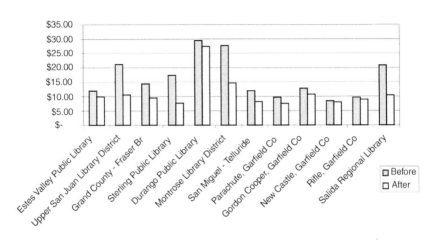

FIGURE 4. Cost for Lending Returnables, Small Public Libraries, Before and After Implementing SWIFT

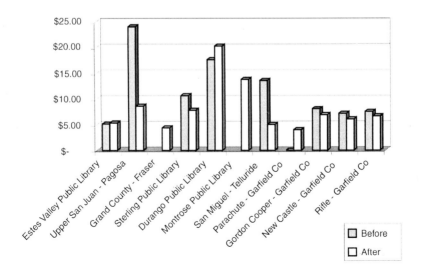

FIGURE 5. Number of Minutes to Complete Requests, Small Public Libraries, Before and After Implementing SWIFT

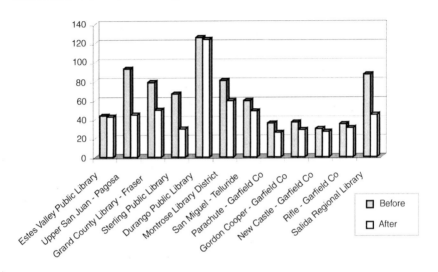

FIGURE 6. Costs for Lending Returnables, Large Public Libraries, Before and After Implementing SWIFT

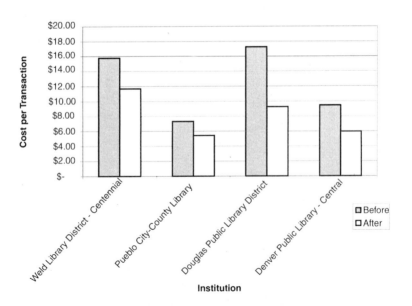

space rental, annual software and hardware maintenance fees, telecommunications, training expenses, and the salaries of three part-time staff. The total costs for SWIFT run about $168,232 annually (see Table 1). SWIFT completed 51,744 transactions between July through December 2002, and the volume for the 2002/03 fiscal year is expected to be double that, for a total of 103,488 transactions. With overall annual costs at $168,232, the cost per transaction for running the system is about $1.63. However, the volume should continue to grow as libraries are added and usage increases. Overall annual costs are not expected to increase, and are more likely to decrease as training needs decline. Operations costs should also decrease with the development of custom reports and availability of new software releases. The cost per transaction for fiscal year 2003-2004 is expected to be about $1.22, reflecting an anticipated increase of 25% in ILL traffic and an overall decrease in personnel costs.

LESSONS LEARNED IN COLORADO

Any project of the size and scope of SWIFT becomes a learning experience. The initial lesson that state library staff relearned was that collaborative statewide software implementation projects always take longer than expected. Originally, the rollout was scheduled with a six-month timeline. In reality, the rollout to early adopters took about a year, and it was nearly two years before a critical mass of libraries was profiled on the system and trained. In addition, some features in the VDX software that

TABLE 1. Annual Cost for SWIFT, 2002-2003

Description	Annual Cost
Space rental–¼ of total space (includes utilities)	$ 972
T1 & Internet access–1/3 of use	$ 2,336
Hardware maintenance for dedicated NT and Unix servers	$ 555
Staff–3 part-time (salary & benefits)	$ 108,399
Training expenses	$ 3,600
Software maintenance	$ 52,370
Total Annual Expenses	**$ 168,232**

the group anticipated would be in the early releases were not available until later in 2003.

One of the reasons that the rollout was slower than anticipated was that the primary target audience was small and medium libraries that were not automated. The biggest challenge in targeting this group was that many of these libraries did not understand the general process of automating ILL and its impact on workflow. Library staff with previous exposure to OCLC's ILL Service understood SWIFT immediately. Those who were still typing paper ALA forms or who relied exclusively on methods such as placing holds in a local catalog to utilize specific lending agreements did not understand the ramifications of fully automating ILL. In some cases, trainers started library staff in group sessions with those from other libraries, and then scheduled several follow-up visits to an individual library to assist with retraining and workflow redesign.

In a distributed system that involves hundreds of small libraries, it is crucial to rely on the political and support structure already in place in the state. In the case of Colorado, there are seven regional multi-type systems and their involvement in the process was critical. State Library staff relied on them to encourage their libraries to join, to automate the small libraries so that their collections would become Z39.50 compliant to build the statewide resource pool, and to provide additional trainers to support the efforts in place. In the High Plains and Plains and Peaks Regional Library Systems, for instance, the ASCC (Automation System Consortia-Colorado) project added over forty small to medium public, school, and special libraries through an expitech (now Dynix) Horizon ASP system. As libraries signed on to the project, they were required to join SWIFT once their catalogs were loaded.

Participants learned that load leveling really does work. The VDX software supports setting up routing groups for lending, and fills the lender string by selecting libraries from the groups in priority order. In Colorado, the groups are based on the seven regional multi-type library systems, so that a rota (FDI's terminology for lender string) is filled first by libraries geographically close, then by other libraries within the next group in priority. This helps distribute the load since library staffs no longer automatically send requests to large libraries first for materials.

The overall statistics for the last six months in operation show new borrowing and lending patterns developing between libraries in the state. VDX provides a statistical spreadsheet (too large to include in this publication) that shows the aggregated traffic in the state as well as all traffic between any two institutions.

It is no longer just the large libraries lending to small libraries. There has been a significant number of small libraries borrowing and lending directly from each other, and regional lending centers are beginning to emerge naturally around the state. While the largest public libraries such as Jefferson County, Arapahoe Library District, and Denver (each serving populations of about 500,000) are understandably the largest net lenders, other public libraries are emerging as significant lenders in their geographic regions. For example, Mesa County Public (serving 116,000), Longmont Public (serving 71,000), and Durango Public (serving 20,000) are borrowing/lending at a ratio of approximately 1:1.

Other libraries, such as San Miguel Library District #1 in Telluride (serving 5,000) and Pitkin County in Aspen (serving 11,000) have a borrowing/lending ratio of approximately 1:2. Some libraries, like Penrose Library District (serving 4,000), have received requests for materials for the first time ever, and have been able to provide them easily through SWIFT. While these lending numbers still do not rival those at the large public libraries, SWIFT allows libraries that never before received interlibrary loan requests to provide services. This development provides some relief for the larger institutions. Indeed, at least two large academic institutions in the state report that they saw a significant reduction in lending to other Colorado libraries last year, which they attribute in part to the SWIFT project.

While the SWIFT project focuses on interlibrary loan transactions, it revealed some inconsistencies in local practice in other areas of library operations. The VDX software relies on the interlibrary loan staff to pick a representative cataloging record from any library; then the system broadcasts a Z39.50 search out to all participating libraries to identify potential lenders. The system uses standard numbers as the searching mechanism for the Z39.50 search, primarily ISBN, ISSN, and LCCN.

As the project rolled out to different libraries, a number of problems with consistency in cataloging practices in individual institutions were identified. For instance, most cataloging for older audiovisual materials does not contain standard numbers, either because they were not available when the materials were originally cataloged or because it was not part of local cataloging practice. In some cases, standard numbers were not included even for monographs due to the original cataloging source. In other cases, the ISBN number was included in the record, but not in the MARC field specifically reserved for it, so a Z39.50 search against the catalog did not retrieve the record. The highest number of unfilled requests in SWIFT continues to be audiovisual materials due to a lack of standard number in the record. Monograph requests that remain unfilled are often due to the fact that the bibliographic record that was selected to generate the search did not contain an ISBN or LCCN.

Any state library agency staff member understands the challenges of working in the multi-type environment: dealing with different types of libraries and trying to find a system that is suitable for all of them. Within the target group, some library staff had difficulty with the software and felt that there were too many choices and options. On the other hand, large academic libraries felt that it was difficult to streamline the workflow enough using the system and that the Web-based version was too slow. Larger research libraries are naturally wedded to the OCLC ILL Service, and in some cases, to circulation-based ILL systems or to Web-based article delivery tied to consortial agreements, because those systems are the most cost effective for them. The intent is not to try to convince them to change to a different ILL system, but rather to figure out how to make new systems fit into their current workflow. Improving SWIFT in ways that will benefit this group is an on-going project, and project coordinators in Wisconsin and New Jersey indicate that they are dealing with similar issues in their statewide initiatives as well (Schatz 2003; Drew 2003).

Institutional libraries, such as those at correctional facilities, created special problems. Due to security concerns, their catalogs cannot be accessed using the Z39.50 server, and there are additional concerns about including them in virtual catalogs and allowing the general public to view the holdings at the individual libraries. As a result, correctional facilities have not been able to take advantage of the same types of streamlining as others participating in SWIFT, although they have found that the system serves them well for requesting materials from libraries outside of the correctional system. One scenario under consideration to alleviate the problems is to create a mirror union catalog of their system outside of their network, available only to other correctional facilities, which would enable them to lend materials easily to each other without comprising Colorado Department of Corrections security.

The final lesson, which was an anticipated outcome, is that interlibrary loan through SWIFT and other intra-state borrowing systems is growing. In addition to SWIFT, there are several other major resource sharing systems in Colorado for intra-state interlibrary loan. Round Robin is a web-based, locally created system used by twelve public libraries. Prospector is an Innovative INN-Reach System used by fifteen (soon to be sixteen) large public and academic libraries for circulation based ILL. PLUS is a second INN-Reach system used by six public libraries. Data for intra-state activity were not available from OCLC for this time period at the writing of this article.

Figure 7 shows the growth in electronic intra-state resource sharing using these systems over the last four years. The data cover July 1 through June 30 of each year. Please note that the earlier years do not necessarily indicate that fewer ILL transactions occurred, but rather that there may have been some traffic occurring via non-electronic means for which data could not be gathered.

The six months of data (July 1, 2002-December 31, 2002) are available for three of these systems (Round Robin data are only provided on an annual basis). The data, reflected in Figure 8, show a dramatic increase in usage.

NEXT STEPS

Membership in the SWIFT project continues to grow, and a number of next steps are planned to improve the system further and continue to reduce the costs of ILL for participating institutions. When the SWIFT pilot service was launched, there were only twenty-nine participating libraries. It has since grown to over 275 (combination of borrowing only, lending only, and both borrowing/lending), and with these new institutions comes the addition of more Z39.50 accessible catalogs. Some of

FIGURE 7. Colorado Interlibrary Lending Transactions by Selected Electronic Means, 1999-2002

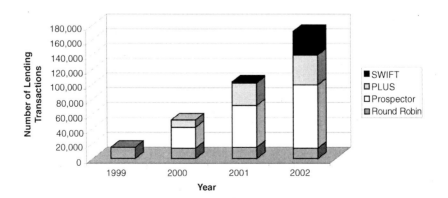

FIGURE 8. Colorado Interlibrary Lending Transactions by Selected Electronic Means, July-December 2002

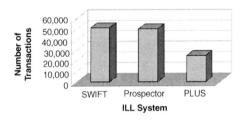

these institutions are larger public libraries that have joined primarily as lenders. As these new resources are added to the pool of available materials, the ILL fill rate should improve.

Additional cost savings at individual libraries can be realized through the implementation of other VDX features. Salida Regional Library System, an OCLC ILL selective user, served as the pilot library for using the ISO ILL 10160/10161 protocol to transfer requests from SWIFT directly up to OCLC. Any requests that are unfilled in Colorado can be automatically transferred by the system to OCLC (treating OCLC as just the next potential lender), where the OCLC ILL system uses the custom holdings to create a lending string and Direct Request functionality to begin the ILL process. The borrowing library then handles all of this OCLC activity using the SWIFT interface. Additional libraries in Colorado have implemented this capability, using it strictly for borrowing at this time, although any library that is an OCLC full or selective user could potentially use the service.

At the Fretwell-Downing User Group meeting at the American Library Association 2003 Midwinter conference, the attendees voted to begin exploring the transfer of requests directly between VDX sites in different states. This functionality was tested during spring 2003, although the policy issues appear to outweigh the technical issues. Making all of the resources from all of the states using VDX software accessible would magnify the pool of resources available directly through SWIFT. In addition, the New Jersey State Library is interested in implementing peer-to-peer sharing between their Auto-Graphics system and Fretwell-Downing VDX once Auto-Graphics completed their implementation of ISO ILL 10160/10161 (which was scheduled for spring 2003).

SWIFT so far has focused primarily on returnable materials. Although the system does support requesting non-returnable items such as photocopies of journal articles, the process is not very efficient since Z39.50 searching is currently based on the ISSN in the serial title record. In June 2003, Fretwell-Downing released a new version of VDX that supports parsing of holdings information in the serial records of the owning libraries. This enhancement allows SWIFT to support requests for journal articles, and to restrict the rota to libraries that subscribed to the journal in the year needed.

Finally, at the end of April 2002, SWIFT quietly released a patron-initiated interface available through the Colorado Virtual Library (CVL). The interface allows patrons to search for material, be authenticated as a valid library card holder, and place a request. This request flows from CVL into their home library's SWIFT account, or if the library has set up their profile to allow it, the system can automatically route the request to the first owning library without any staff intervention. This service could significantly reduce staff time spent on managing the ILL process. Currently, eight libraries have released the service to their patrons.

One unexpected event caused a slowdown in the promotion of patron-initiated requesting to potential users. In May 2002, as part of a package of state budget cuts for FY02-03, the governor of Colorado zeroed out funding that amounted to approximately $4.3 million in funds that would have gone to support building collections and resource sharing in the state, including support for the Colorado Resource Center (Denver Public Library has provided this service on a contract basis in the past). It is unclear exactly what the impact of these cuts on resource sharing in Colorado will be. The State Library will be tracking usage of SWIFT as well as patterns of resource sharing throughout the year. The cuts did slow down further adoption of patron-initiated ILL due to the fact that some level of reimbursement could no longer be promised to net lenders in the state, and release of patron-initiated service generally increases ILL traffic overall.

CONCLUSION

Like any software implementation project, SWIFT has had its rough spots during training, and new software releases are always slower than anticipated. In general, however, the project has been quite successful. The target audiences–small and medium size libraries–have saved both time and money by using SWIFT to automate their interlibrary loan processes. As anticipated, the lending load throughout the state is shifting slowly, and libraries that had never before been asked to lend their materials are eagerly providing that service to their peer institutions. Finding the right solutions for all sizes and types of institutions in a state is always challenging, but progress continues towards adding services to SWIFT that appeal to broader audiences. The adoption of new services, such as peer-to-peer requesting between states and better support for non-returnable borrowing, will help pique the interest of institutions not currently participating in the service.

But most importantly, the SWIFT Project has become more than just a resource sharing project. It has moved into library development. It has helped staff at small and medium libraries to develop new skills and to improve services to their users, as well as to become active participants in, and an integral part of, resource sharing in Colorado.

AUTHOR NOTE

For more information on the SWIFT service, contact Brenda Bailey-Hainer at <bailey_b@cde.state.co.us>, and visit the information webpage for the project at: <http://www.aclin.org/swift>. Additional information on the Colorado Virtual Library is available at <http://www.aclin.org>.

NOTES

Drew, Sally. 2003. Telephone interview by author, 7 February. Denver, CO.

Fong, Yem. 1997. *ACLIN Patron Initiated Electronic Interlibrary Loan System. Final Report, April 9, 1997.* Unpublished manuscript.

Institute of Library and Museum Services. 2003. *Grants to State Library Agencies Website* <http://www.imls.gov/grants/library/lib_gsla.asp>.

Kroe, E., P. Garner, and C. Sheckells. 2001. *State Library Agencies: Fiscal Year 2000* (NCES 2000-302). U.S. Department of Education, National Center for Education Statistics. Washington, D.C.

Madsen, Jean. 2001. *SWIFT Workflow and Cost Analysis.* Unpublished manuscript.

Schatz, Scherelene. 2003. Telephone interview by author, 7 February. Denver, CO.

U.S. Department of Education, National Center for Education Statistics. 1999. *State Library Agencies, Fiscal Year 1998* (NCES 2000-318), Elaine Kroe, Survey Manager. U.S. Department of Education, National Center for Education Statistics. Washington, D.C.

U.S. Department of Education, National Center for Education Statistics. 2000. *State Library Agencies, Fiscal Year 1999* (NCES 2000-374), Elaine Kroe, Survey Manager. U.S. Department of Education, National Center for Education Statistics. Washington, D.C.

U.S. Department of Education, National Center for Education Statistics. 2002. *State Library Agencies: Fiscal Year 2001 (NCES 2003-309),* by Barbara Holton, Elaine Kroe, Patricia O'Shea, Cindy Sheckells, Suzanne Dorinski, and Michael Freeman.

Major Copyright Issues
in Academic Libraries:
Legal Implications
of a Digital Environment

Donna L. Ferullo

SUMMARY. This paper provides an overview of some of the major copyright issues for libraries in a digital environment. It explores how statutory and case law determine the path libraries must take to accomplish their mission. Copyright law is complex and ambiguous. It poses many challenges for librarians, but it is crucial that librarians have a basic understanding of the various provisions of the law in order to make informed decisions. However, the law is only one part of the equation. The interpretation of the law by the courts must also be constantly evaluated for potential impact to libraries. *[Article copies available for a fee from The Haworth Document Delivery Service: 1-800-HAWORTH. E-mail address: <docdelivery@haworthpress.com> Website: <http://www.HaworthPress.com> © 2004 by The Haworth Press, Inc. All rights reserved.]*

KEYWORDS. Copyright, copyright law and legislation, copyright and libraries, DMCA, TEACH Act

Donna L. Ferullo is Director and Assistant Professor, University Copyright Office, Purdue University Libraries (E-mail: ferullo@purdue.edu).

[Haworth co-indexing entry note]: "Major Copyright Issues in Academic Libraries: Legal Implications of a Digital Environment." Ferullo, Donna L. Co-published simultaneously in *Journal of Library Administration* (The Haworth Information Press, an imprint of The Haworth Press, Inc.) Vol. 40, No. 1/2, 2004, pp. 23-40; and: *The Changing Landscape for Electronic Resources: Content, Access, Delivery, and Legal Issues* (ed: Yem S. Fong, and Suzanne M. Ward) The Haworth Information Press, an imprint of The Haworth Press, Inc., 2004, pp. 23-40. Single or multiple copies of this article are available for a fee from The Haworth Document Delivery Service [1-800-HAWORTH, 9:00 a.m. - 5:00 p.m. (EST). E-mail address: docdelivery@haworthpress.com].

23

INTRODUCTION

Academic librarians face complex issues and challenges in navigating the maze that is the copyright landscape. Some of the issues are obvious, but others are far more subtle, particularly in a digital environment. Issues that invoke confusion and concern as to the applicability of the copyright law include e-reserves, licensing, document delivery, and fair use. The mission of academic libraries in the most simplistic language is to provide their constituents access to information anywhere and at anytime. However, how a library accomplishes that mission within the parameters of the copyright law is usually debatable and is sometimes dependent upon each university's interpretation of the law.

Due to recent legislation and court cases, the message in some areas of copyright law is ambiguous at best. Also, United States copyright law does not exist in a vacuum. It is very much driven by international copyright law. The rapid advancement of technology allows for invisible borders. International partnerships are formed that even ten years ago would have been inconceivable. As the United States becomes a signatory to many international treaties, the U.S. laws must change in order to be in compliance with the treaties and in copyright harmony with the international community. The international treaties are the world powers' attempt to standardize copyright. To understand the fundamental concept of copyright, one must approach it from a macro level before one can apply it at a micro level.

COPYRIGHT BASICS

The word "copyright" and the phrase "intellectual property" are sometime used interchangeably, but in actuality copyright law is one arm of the intellectual property triumvirate. The other two arms are patent law and trademark law. There has always been much philosophical legal debate over the validity of the term "intellectual property" as it relates to other types of property such as personal and real. Suffice to say that intellectual property and as such copyright can be transferred to another person or entity and can also be part of an estate and disposed of via a will or trust. It is recognized as property and as such a valuable commodity. The stakes are high and have become even more so in a digital world. All one has to do to see the impact is to look at the proliferation of pirated works, particularly of sound recordings and movies. The recording industry and the motion picture association do not take copyright infringement lightly. Much of the new legislation and case law has been dictated by such influential industries.

The value of copyright was recognized as early as the United States' struggle for independence. The Constitution states, "The Congress shall have power . . . to promote the progress of science and useful arts by securing for limited times to authors and inventors the exclusive right to their respective writing and discoveries." Copyright law is all about balance. Our forefathers' intent was to balance the rights of the author with the rights of the public to use the information freely. The premise of copyright is that authors need an incentive to create works and the incentive is to allow the authors to have exclusive rights to their works for a limited period of time. The authors' exclusive rights include the right to reproduce and distribute their work, to publicly display and perform their work and to create derivative works. It is assumed that during that limited period of time authors will be compensated for the use of their work. Once the limited time has expired, the work becomes part of the public domain to be freely used by anyone. Authors are then justly rewarded in two ways; first by the compensation and second by the knowledge that their creative work contributes to the greater intellectual good of mankind.

However, there are exemptions to the authors' exclusive rights. The law recognizes that in certain instances the public should benefit from the authors' work without paying royalties or seeking permission before the copyright term has expired. There are specific exemptions for libraries and education, but probably one of the most used exemptions is fair use. Each exemption will be addressed later in the article.

The last major overhaul of the copyright law occurred in 1976. At that time the balance began to shift more in favor of the copyright holder. One of the most important changes to the law was the dissolution of the formal copyright registration requirement. Works that were original and fixed in a tangible medium of expression received automatic copyright protection. Authors no longer had to register their work.

The law has been amended since 1976. In recent years the most noteworthy amendments include the Digital Millennium Copyright Act (DMCA), the Sonny Bono Copyright Term Extension Act (C.T.E.A.) and the Technology, Education and Copyright Harmonization (TEACH) Act. With the passage of each of these recent amendments, the balance is weighing more in favor of the copyright owner. The exemptions then become more crucial than ever.

Case law is also having a significant impact in shaping the interpretation of copyright. The courts have had to apply traditional copyright in a digital environment. The result has been the introduction of new buzz-words such as e-copyright or digital copyright.

LEGISLATION AND CASE LAW

Digital Millennium Copyright Act

The Digital Millennium Copyright Act (DMCA) was passed in 1998 to address the use of copyright in a digital world. The DMCA was a direct result of what was happening in the international community. In 1996, the United States became a party to the World Intellectual Property Organization (WIPO) treaties; thus U.S. laws needed to change to reflect international copyright law.

There are five major sections to the DMCA, but the most controversial is the anti-circumvention provision. This section prohibits the circumvention of protection technologies to access copyrighted works. It also prohibits the manufacturing of technological devices that would circumvent the protection. Nonprofit libraries and educational institutions are exempt from this section if they gain access to the protected material in order to evaluate it for acquisition. Under this new law the Register of Copyright is required to conduct proceedings to review and evaluate the effect the anti-circumvention provision has had and to recommend to the Librarian of Congress classes of works that should be exempted from the anti-circumvention provision of the DMCA. The first review is currently being conducted. The anti-circumvention provision of the DMCA did not go into effect until two years after the passage of the Act. The first review was structured to take place two years after the provision went into effect, beginning in 2002. Reviews will take place every three years hereafter.

The anti-circumvention provision has already given rise to three noteworthy cases. The three cases have a common denominator and that is the restriction of research and academic freedom, which is in essence a direct contradiction of the intent of our forefathers who wanted to encourage creativity, not stifle it.

The first case involves Ed Felten, a Princeton professor, who accepted a challenge from the Recording Industry Association of America (RIAA) to crack the new security protection devices that had been installed on CDs. The security was intended to prevent CDs from being illegally copied and shared via file sharing services such as the now defunct Napster.

Professor Felten did indeed crack the code and planned to announce his research findings at a professional conference. The RIAA got word of the professor's plan and sent him a letter reminding him of the anti-circumvention provision of the DMCA. Professor Felten thought it prudent not to release his findings at that time. The RIAA played the traditional legal cat-and-mouse game of subtly hinting that legal action might follow if the code was revealed. Professor Felten took a proactive stance and requested the court prevent the RIAA from suing him (Foster, June 7, 2001). The case was dismissed because there was no actual legal case or legal controversy, merely preliminary posturing (Foster, November 29, 2001). Eventually the research findings were presented and the RIAA did not sue Professor Felten. It is my guess that the RIAA was besieged by protests and decided that the continued negative publicity would be more costly than suing the professor given the circumstances.

Another case that somewhat parallels the Felten case is *United States v. ElcomSoft*. In this case Dmitry Sklyarov, an employee of the Russian company ElcomSoft, who lived and worked in Russia, cracked the technological protection code of Adobe e-books. Mr. Sklyarov made an ill-fated decision to attend a hacker conference in Las Vegas where he would present his research and promote ElcomSoft's product. Adobe became aware of Mr. Sklyarov's planned trip to the United States and alerted the Department of Justice. Mr. Sklyarov presented his findings at the conference and was immediately arrested for violating the anti-circumvention provision of the DMCA (Harmon & Lee, 2001). What is quite noteworthy about this case is that this was the first time that criminal charges were brought under the DMCA. Most cases are civil and involve only money damages, not jail time.

The research community in all sectors was outraged at the arrest of Mr. Sklyarov and picketed Adobe headquarters in California. Adobe quickly realized that it might have acted hastily and the wiser course of action would have been to pursue other avenues of recourse. However, it was too late to turn back and also out of Adobe's hands. Since it was a criminal violation of a federal law only the United States government could drop the charges and they chose not to do so. Mr. Sklyarov agreed to cooperate with the authorities and was given immunity in exchange for his testimony against ElcomSoft.

In December 2002 a jury found ElcomSoft not guilty of the charges leveled against them (Bowman, 2002). The Court instructed the jury that in order to find the company guilty of violating the DMCA, they needed to look at the state of mind of ElcomSoft to determine whether or not they willfully intended to violate the law. The decision in this case will certainly make legal history by defining just how far the criminal tentacles of the DMCA can reach; it also sets the legal standard by which other criminal cases brought under the DMCA will have to meet.

The third case involves the motion picture industry and DVDs. The DVD technology does not work with a Linux operating system. Eric Corley, the editor of *2600 Magazine* published the computer code called DeCSS that bypasses the DVD protection and allows motion pictures to be viewed using the Linux operating system. The code cracking software program was widely distributed via the magazine and on their web site. Members of the Motion Picture Association of America (MPAA) filed a civil suit against the magazine and Mr. Corley in January 2000 for violating the anti-circumvention provision of the DMCA. This was the first civil case brought under the DMCA.

The Court ruled in favor of the motion picture industry but the opinion by the judge was quite a red flag for future litigation (Hansen, 2001). Judge Kaplan for the United States District Court for the Southern District of New York ruled that posting the DeCSS code on a web site or linking to the code was a violation of the copyright law. The decision in the case opens a Pandora's box regarding linking to web sites that might potentially post illegal content. The ramifications of this decision are enormous.

All three cases have certainly showcased the chilling effect of the DMCA on research and academic freedom. One of the by-products of these cases is the reluctance and oftentimes refusal of international researchers to announce their findings and attend conferences in the United States due to the restrictions and penalties imposed by the DMCA (Bray, 2001). The results of these cases also highlight the shifting of the copyright balance to favor the content owner to the detriment of the public.

Another major provision to the DMCA is the limited liability clause for online-service providers. Congress recognized that companies such as America Online (AOL) and institutions of higher education that provide Internet access and space on their servers should not be held liable in certain instances for users who infringe on someone's copyright since they do not own, direct, or monitor the content. The copyright infringement and subsequent liability are the responsibility of the user.

To qualify as an online service provider (OSP), there are multiple requirements that must be met. The OSP must designate an agent, who is registered with the United States Copyright Office, to receive notifications of alleged infringement; remove the infringing material; possibly disable the alleged infringer's access to the network if needed; and implement a policy that informs users of the potential actions that would be taken by the OSP in cases of infringement. This section of the DMCA has been considered in many ways a boon for higher education in terms of restricting universities' liability, but in recent months the recording industry has ratcheted up their demands that universities take a more proactive role in monitoring and restricting peer-to-peer file sharing which is where the majority of the piracy occurs (Carlson, 2003). Generally, universities and colleges either designate an agent or develop procedures to handle notifications of alleged copyright infringement from entities such as the RIAA. The notification identifies an IP address, but not the name of the alleged infringer. Upon notification of a potential infringement, universities generally remove the material from their server, and identify the person responsible for posting the material. If that person is a student, then the Dean of Students is usually involved in a wide range of disciplinary procedures. Once the material has been removed, there is generally no further action taken by the complainant. The complainant is generally satisfied with the removal of the infringing material and does not generally request the university to identify the alleged infringer.

However, the RIAA has recently tested the limits of the OSP provision of the DMCA and has won a major legal victory. The RIAA sued Verizon Communications, an Internet service provider, to reveal the identity of one of their customers who was allegedly illegally distributing copyrighted music. Verizon argued that they were merely a conduit and did not have servers where customers could store their information. Verizon's role was to simply provide access to the Internet. Verizon also claimed that it would be a violation of their subscriber's right to privacy and would also deprive them of due process. The Court disagreed and ruled that Verizon must provide the RIAA with the identity of the subscriber (Harmon, 2003). This ruling peels away one more layer of protection for the copyright user. The ruling in the Verizon case potentially poses a greater risk of liability for universities and their students.

The proliferation of illegal file sharing has even prompted some of the major higher education organizations such as the National Association of State Universities and Land-Grant Colleges, the American Council on Education, the American Association of State Colleges and Universities, and the National Association of Independent Colleges and Universities to send a letter to the presidents of all American colleges to be proactive in reducing and hopefully even stopping the piracy of movies and songs (Kiernan, 2002). The potential for future major litigation between one of the powerful arts industries and a university is very real.

Academia is walking a tightrope in trying to comply with the law and, in certain instances, with the demands of the RIAA without impinging on the academic freedom of students and faculty. One wonders whether this action is similar to the Felten case with a subtle threat being issued or is the RIAA looking for a piracy poster child at a major university or college that does not join their cause? As the stakes get higher for all parties, the protection offered by the OSP provision of the DMCA is now being put to the test

There is also a DMCA provision for libraries, which allows them to make digital copies of deteriorating works for preservation purposes. The caveat to that expansion of rights is that the digital copy may only be used on the library premises. The specific restriction to library premises is very troubling. After all how does one define library premises in a virtual library? Libraries are also allowed to make copies of works if the current work is in a format that is technologically obsolete. Congress took this opportunity to clarify that all copies made under the library exemption, which is section 108 of the copyright law, must include a formal copyright notice or a statement on the copyright law and its protection of certain works.

The DMCA is quite complex and is just beginning to be interpreted by the courts. All the challenges to the DMCA and the outcomes of the review process by the Librarian of Congress need to be closely monitored.

Sonny Bono Copyright Term Extension Act

The Sonny Bono Copyright Term Extension Act (C.T.E.A) was also passed in 1998. This new law extended the term of copyright an additional twenty years, from life of the author plus fifty years to life of the author plus seventy years. Protection for corporate authors was extended from seventy-five to ninety-five years from the date of publication. The extension included copyright in existing works as well as any new works.

This piece of legislation was the direct result of the powerful Disney lobbyists. The copyright for Mickey Mouse, one of Disney's most famous and lucrative creations, was about to expire and enter the public domain. The additional twenty years ensures that the public cannot use Disney's creations without financial gain for Disney.

The Copyright Term Extension Act has an impact not only on Disney, but also on all the other works that were scheduled to enter the public domain. The C.T.E.A. was challenged by Eric Eldred who was in the process of creating a public domain database of famous literary works.

Mr. Eldred claimed that the new law went too far and that it violated the intent of our forefathers by extending the term of copyright beyond what a reasonable person would consider a limited time (Foster, October 25, 2002). This instance was not the first time that Congress bowed to powerful interest groups by extending copyright protection, but Mr. Eldred argues that it should be the last. The lower courts ruled against Mr. Eldred but the United States Supreme Court agreed to hear the case.

In January 2003, the Supreme Court issued their decision in the Eldred case and upheld the constitutionality of the Copyright Term Extension Act. The opinion by Justice Ruth Bader Ginsburg states "In sum, we find that the C.T.E.A. is a rational enactment; we are not at liberty to second-guess Congressional determinations and policy judgments of this order, however debatable and arguably unwise they may be" (New York Times, 2003). The Court also addressed the challenge by the plaintiffs that the C.T.E.A. impinged upon First Amendment and free speech rights. Justice Ginsburg summarily dismissed that claim by reasoning that the "copyright law contains built-in First Amendment accommodations including the concept of fair use" (Greenhouse, 2003).

The decision was a severe blow to advocates of the public domain and truly limited copyright terms. However, it was a major victory for corporations like Disney and for other entities such as the recording and motion picture industries. The Court indicated that Congress has the power to keep extending the duration of copyright as long as it is not specified as perpetual. Any time period can be considered limited under this ruling, a definition that does not bode well for users of copyrighted works. The Court's decision has shifted the balance more than ever in favor of the copyright holder.

Technology, Education and Copyright Harmonization Act

Another major piece of legislation entitled the Technology, Education and Copyright Harmonization Act (TEACH) was signed into law by President Bush in November 2002. The TEACH Act totally rewrites the distance education section of the education exemption. The intent of the TEACH Act was to attempt to equalize distance education with classroom teaching. The new law applies to the transmission of digital works.

Prior to the new law, all displays of materials were allowed to be transmitted to distance education students but only performances of non-dramatic literary and musical works were allowed. There were also other restrictions as to where the transmission could be received and who could receive it.

The new law still allows for complete works of non-dramatic literary and musical works to be transmitted but now also permits limited and reasonable portions of performances of all other works including audiovisuals and sound recordings. Displays have been limited to an amount that is comparable to what would take place in a live classroom setting.

Works that are not permitted to be transmitted include materials that were produced primarily for instruction via digital networks. Course packs, textbooks, and other works that are typically purchased by students for use in one or more class sessions are also prohibited from being transmitted. The intent of these legislative restrictions is to protect the educational market for publishers and other content owners.

However, there are many requirements that must be met by universities and their information technology departments before faculty can avail themselves of the revised exemption. Some of the requirements are not technologically possible, but some can be accomplished via functions of different courseware programs. The TEACH Act applies to only accredited nonprofit educational institutions or a government body. Universities are required to institute copyright policies and provide informational material on copyright to faculty, relevant staff, and students. There is also a provision in this new law that requires a notice to students stating that their course materials may be subject to copyright protection.

The TEACH Act is quite complex, ambiguous, and has many gray areas. As is the case in many of the amendments to the copyright law, it will take litigation to interpret the various provisions.

DIGITAL COPYRIGHT

In 2001 the United States Supreme Court handed down a major decision in the case of *New York Times v. Tasini* that has influenced and in part defined the digital copyright landscape. The case began in 1993 when freelance authors represented by Jonathan Tasini sued *The New York Times* and other publishers for copyright infringement.

The New York Times had compiled databases of the freelancers' articles that had previously been published in their print publications. The publishers defended their actions by claiming that the articles included in the databases were revisions, which was authorized in their contracts with the authors. However, the authors vociferously disagreed and argued that electronic databases allowed their articles to be accessed individually and not as part of the whole publication in which they were originally published, thus infringing on their exclusive rights granted under the copyright law to reproduce and distribute their works.

The District Court ruled in favor of the publishers. The Appeals Court overturned the District Court and ruled in favor of the authors, and the United States Supreme Court sided with the Appeals Court and ruled in favor of the authors.

The outcome has been the removal of freelance articles from many of the major databases. *The New York Times* requested that all freelancers covered under the case sign an amended contract that would allow *The Times* to use their works in the databases but without further remuneration. If the freelancers did not comply, then their works would be removed. Many authors did not succumb to the strong arm tactics employed by *The Times*; thus their articles were removed. The fight for appropriate payment is still being litigated. However, *The Times* and many other publishers in the early stages of the *Tasini* litigation changed the boilerplate contracts that they present to authors to include language that would give them all rights including electronic rights.

Another case that did not garner as much publicity as the *Tasini* case but that certainly solidifies the distinction between traditional copyright and e-copyright is *Rosetta Books v. Random House*. The facts of the case are similar to *Tasini* in that authors signed contracts that allowed Random House to publish and distribute their works in print. However, the contracts were silent on the issue of electronic rights. Rosetta Books then entered into contracts with the authors to publish e-versions of their works. Random House claimed that they had all rights including electronic to the works and thus Rosetta was infringing on their copyright. The Court sided with Rosetta and ruled that unless the contract specifically includes electronic works then the electronic rights are separate and can be contracted to another party. Random House appealed the ruling and lost the appeal (*Software Law Bulletin*, 2002). Random House and Rosetta Books then reached an agreement whereby Rosetta Books will have an exclusive license with Random House to publish specific works as e-books (*Intellectual Property Litigation Reporter*, 2002).

The moral of the story is that in essence the Courts have recognized both a print copyright and a digital copyright. In most cases the defining factor is the specificity of the contract and the court's interpretation of it. This is a good lesson in Contracts 101 where contracts or licenses for use of works must be very specific as to what precisely is allowed and in what manner.

The above legislation and case law define a new era on the copyright landscape. The courts have made a distinction between electronic and print rights, thus adding the phrase "digital copyright" to the intellectual property vocabulary. However, some of the recent legislation such as the DMCA and the TEACH Act attempt to have digital works mirror print works when, by their very nature, they have different capabilities and capacities for use. Until Congress recognizes that there is a real distinction in the use of each type of work, the courts will be inundated attempting to define the differences and appropriate applications. They are basically trying to put a square peg in a round hole.

COPYRIGHT LAW EXEMPTIONS

There are two major exemptions generally used by the higher education community; the education exemption and the fair use exemption. There is also an exemption for libraries. The exemptions are all independent of each other, so if one is not appropriate for the use of a work then there is no legal reason why the other exemption should not be utilized if applicable.

The education exemption is divided into two sections: classroom teaching and distance education. As long as the work that is being used in the classroom is relevant to the curriculum, then all types of works can be either displayed or performed.

The distance education section has been totally revised by the TEACH Act which was discussed earlier in this article. Suffice to say that there are now many more hoops that faculty must go through to transmit digital works for distance education or for courses with a digital component. The scope of the exemption is broader in some respects, but the additional requirements that must be in place to use the exemption may dissuade many academics from taking advantage of this exemption.

Fair use appears still to be the exemption of choice or maybe more by default in most cases. The fair use four-factor test is technologically neutral which makes the application of the exemption much easier for many people. This exemption also directly parallels our forefathers' intent to strike a balance between the users of the work and the owners of the work.

The four factors: purpose and character; nature; amount; and market effect are first evaluated separately and either weigh in favor of fair use or weigh against fair use. When there are four factors or even three factors in favor of fair use, the decision is clear. However, difficulties arise when it is a tie with two factors weighing in favor of fair use and two factors weighing against fair use. It is important that the person making the decision makes a good faith determination that the use is ultimately fair use under the copyright law. If there should be a lawsuit for copyright infringement, damages can be somewhat mitigated if the individual can show that he understood the four factors and can articulate the rationale for his decision.

One of the major myths associated with this exemption is that all educational use is fair use. If a work is to be used for educational purposes then the first factor of the fair use test, purpose and character, would weigh in favor of the use. However, there are three other factors that must be applied before a determination can be made as to whether the use is fair.

As more and more requirements and restrictions are placed on other exemptions, fair use is sometimes the only viable option. It becomes more invaluable every day.

The library exemption allows copying for various purposes such as interlibrary loan, personal use, and preservation. There are requirements that must be met in order for libraries to utilize the exemption but generally academic libraries usually meet the qualifications with little difficulty.

LIBRARY ISSUES

Some of the major copyright issues facing libraries have some type of digital component. As a result of the new laws and recent court decisions, copyright compliance for libraries in the digital environment poses constant challenges.

E-reserves is certainly a good example of the conundrum that librarians face in trying to provide the most up-to-date and best information to their patrons in an efficacious manner while trying to comply with the many ambiguous provisions of the copyright law.

The major stumbling block to an e-reserves program is initially not the copyright law itself, but rather the difficulty in establishing a policy to deal with the copyright issues. In many colleges and universities there is no clear cut copyright policy and so many librarians are reluctant to undertake the risk of liability of having their university sued for copyright infringement. However, if an e-reserves program is to be implemented, a decision has to be made as to how copyrighted materials will be handled.

Some librarians play it safe and request permission for any copyrighted work that they put on e-reserve. Others only use works that are in the public domain. The fair use exemption plays a major role in e-reserves for some institutions. Some libraries have made the decision that all first time use is fair use and any subsequent use requires permission, while others have determined that if they own the material then the use is fair no matter how many times the work is placed on reserve. Links to full-text databases that are licensed by the library are generally considered to provide easy access and worry-free copyright. A conscious decision must be made as to which choice is the best for all parties concerned.

The enactment of the TEACH Act has a potential impact on e-reserves. As mentioned earlier in this article, the TEACH exemption involves transmitting digital works. Should all the parameters required by the TEACH Act be in place, then the exemption can be utilized. However, librarians need to be cognizant of the multiple restrictions on the types of materials that can be transmitted. Materials that could be considered supplementary to the course content do not qualify for the TEACH Act exemption.

The TEACH Act is also very specific about converting analog materials to digital. The conversion can only take place if no digital version is available to the institution or if the work has technological protections and is not subject to the coverage under TEACH. The amount that can be converted must be limited to the amount that is needed and that would be comparable to what takes place in a live classroom setting.

Even though the TEACH exemption is available, it is quite complex with many requirements and constraints. It also depends upon other parts of the university instituting policies and procedures before the exemption can be used. It appears that the fair use exemption is more of a viable option given its flexibility.

Licensing is an area where librarians can in essence negotiate the terms of copyright. Licenses are contracts, which can trump copyright. In other words a license agreement can allow a copyright holder to grant to the other party some or all of the same exclusive rights that the owner has, such as reproduction and distribution rights.

License agreements can range from the simple to the complex, from one page to ten or more pages. The more sophisticated licenses have very similar boilerplate language. The majority of terms in license agreements have some negotiable points. Libraries as the consumers or customers can and should dictate many of the terms of these agreements.

Document delivery issues are many times intertwined with license agreements. Libraries are bound by the terms of the agreement; however, there can be a lack of communication between staff that provide document delivery services and staff that negotiate and sign the agreements. It is necessary for all parties to be aware of the content and scope of the agreement to maximize the use of the materials.

Because of the ease of duplication and distribution of electronic content, publishers have implemented strict measures in an attempt to prevent copyright infringement. Many licenses for electronic resources include a provision that allows ILL departments to make a paper copy of the material, but not to distribute the document electronically to the patron. The limitation imposed by such licenses can have a detrimental effect to the fundamental mission of a library. Therefore, it is prudent to try and negotiate different terms in the license that are favorable to multiple uses of works regardless of the format or mode of delivery. Most libraries have safeguards in place to prevent unauthorized access to copyrighted materials. Publishers need to be better educated on the different policies and procedures that libraries have established to protect their intellectual property. The publishers' fear of intellectual property theft might then be somewhat alleviated.

There is a new licensing player in the field that merits mention and consideration. Creative Commons was founded in 2001. Its "goal is to develop a rich repository of high-quality works in a variety of media and to promote an ethos of sharing, public education, and creative interactivity" (Creative Commons, 2003). This new venture provides some boilerplate language for licenses that allows copyright holders to retain some rights in their works but also allows the public access, generally without compensation to them. It is not quite public domain material but certainly offers copyright holders multiple suggestions and options in how best to retain some rights but still allow their works to benefit the public.

The *Tasini* decision has wreaked havoc in libraries, particularly for document delivery services. Publishers have removed articles from databases making it virtually impossible to access some works, particularly if there is no print version. Removing works that might be subject to potential copyright infringement litigation is far easier to do in an electronic environment than a print one. Libraries and research institutions now have to deal with a here today gone tomorrow collection. A library's cache of information is now transient.

With the Supreme Court ruling against Eldred and upholding the C.T.E.A., libraries now have to deal with the fact that there is no turning back the clock on copyright duration. For a while there was hope that many works would enter the public domain if the C.T.E.A. had been declared unconstitutional. The only fairly safe rule of thumb to follow is that works published prior to 1923 are in the public domain.

CONCLUSION

Copyright law is not static. It changes continuously with each new amendment and court case. There are several areas that bear close scrutiny.

The first is the controversy swirling around the issue of linking to Internet sites. In the *DeCSS* case, Judge Kaplan set a standard for linking to sites that post the DeCSS code, which is a violation of the DMCA. Potential future litigation could certainly include defining the legality and parameters of linking, be it linking to sites that allegedly contain illegal material; deep linking whereby links bypass a home page to go directly to the information; or a direct link imbedded in a work. There has been some major litigation on linking issues in Europe but relatively very few cases in the United States (Delio, 2003).

The second area that should be closely monitored is legislation submitted to Congress. There will be many bills introduced that would strengthen the copyright holder's rights and by doing so shrink the rights available to the users of copyrighted materials. The opponents to such legislation are vocal and the ensuing debates should be enlightening.

The key strategy for librarians is engagement at the university-wide level. Copyright by virtue of law and necessity has become a hot topic at most universities. It is in the library's best interest to become actively involved in drafting university copyright policies. Librarians have much at stake in such policies and their contributions at the discussion, drafting, and implementation stages can offer a unique perspective.

Licenses are drafted and negotiated in both the libraries and in university contract offices. Librarians need to be active participants in all licenses that affect their library. This is the time when copyright can be defined and rights can be negotiated.

A final recommendation is for librarians to become as knowledgeable as possible about copyright. The rapid pace of technological innovation constantly challenges the traditional application of the copyright law. Librarians are generally on the cutting edge of such new technology and have the opportunity and responsibility to assist in educating their campuses about the impact of copyright law on libraries, particularly in a digital environment.

NOTES

Bowman, Lisa M. "ElcomSoft verdict: Not guilty." *CNET News.com* 17 December 2002. <http://news.com.com/2100-1023-978176.html>.

Bray, Hiawatha. "Silence of a code cracker." *Boston Globe* 16 August 2001. <http://digitalmass.boston.com/news/globe_tech/upgrade/2001/0816.html>.

Carlson, Scott. "Recording industry plans to accelerate complaints about illegal file sharing." *Chronicle of Higher Education* 3 January 2003: A38.

Creative Commons. 31 January 2003. <http://creativecommons.org/learn/aboutus/>.

Delio, Michelle. "This is your deep link on P2P." *Wired News* 17 January 2003. <http://www.wired.com/news/pollitics/0,1283,57230,00html>.

Foster, Andrea L. "Princeton U. computer scientist sues for permission to speak out at conference." *Chronicle of Higher Education.* 7 June 2001. <http://chronicle.com/free/2001/06/201060701t.htm>.

Foster, Andrea L. "Judge dismisses digital-copyright lawsuit by Princeton professor." *Chronicle of Higher Education.* 29 November 2001. <http://chronicle.com/free/2001/11/2001112901t.htm>.

Foster, Andrea L. "A Bookworm's battle." *Chronicle of Higher Education* 25 October 2002: A35.

Greenhouse, Linda. "20-Year extension of copyright is upheld." *New York Times,* 16 January 2003: A22.

Hansen, Evan. "Ban on DVD-cracking code upheld." *CNET News.com* 28 November 2001. <http://news.cnet.com/news/0-1005-200-8011238.html?tag=prntfr>.

Harmon, Amy. "Verizon ordered to give identity of Net subscriber." *The New York Times* 22 January 2003: C1.

Harmon, Amy and Lee, Jennifer. "Arrest raises stakes in battle over copyright." *The New York Times* 7 July 2001: 1.

Kiernan, Vincent. "Higher-education organizations urge a crackdown on illegal file sharing." *Chronicle of Higher Education* 10 October 2002. <http://chronicle.com/free/2002/10/2002101002t.htm>.

New York Times. "Court majority says it won't second-guess Congress." *The New York Times* 16 January 2003: A22.

"Random House fails to win reversal of injunction in 'e-books' case." *Software Law Bulletin* 15 no. 12 (2002): 14.

"Random House, Rosetta settle e-book case." *Intellectual Property Litigation Reporter* 9 no. 17 (2002): 7.

LAWS

Copyright Law 17 U.S.C. §§ 101 *et seq.*

Digital Millennium Copyright Act of 1998, 112 Stat. 2860 (1998).

Sonny Bono Copyright Term Extension Act of 1998, 112 Stat. 2827 (1998).

Technology, Education and Copyright Harmonization Act of 2002, 116 Stat. 1910 (2002).

U.S. Constitution. Art I, §8, cl. 8.

CASES

Eldred v. Ashcroft, 123 S.Ct. 769; 2003 U.S. LEXIS 751 (2003).

New York Times Co. v. Tasini, 533 U.S. 483 (2001).

Random House v. Rosetta Books, 283 F.3d 490 (2nd Cir. 2002).
United States v. ElcomSoft Co. Ltd., No. CR 01-20138 RMW, United States District Court for the Northern District of California, San Jose Division, 2002.
Universal City v. Corley, 273 F.3d 429 (2nd Cir. 2001).
Verizon Internet Services, Inc. v. Recording Industry Association of America, 2003 U.S. Dist. LEXIS 681.

Licensed to ILL:
A Beginning Guide
to Negotiating E-Resources Licenses
to Permit Resource Sharing

Jeffrey C. Carrico
Kathleen L. Smalldon

SUMMARY. Electronic resources are more prolific than ever. As an increasing number of publishers move to electronic format, the number of licenses grows proportionately. In universities, these licenses may be negotiated by someone with little or no library experience, or by someone who may focus on other aspects of the licenses. This paper promotes and heightens the negotiator's awareness of interlibrary loan (ILL) considerations, and advocates direct intervention by ILL staff in the licensing process. Northern Arizona University Library's experience and negotiation methods with respect to interlibrary loan language and procedures are discussed. *[Article copies available for a fee from The Haworth Document Delivery Service: 1-800-HAWORTH. E-mail address: <docdelivery@haworthpress.com> Website: <http://www.HaworthPress.com> © 2004 by The Haworth Press, Inc. All rights reserved.]*

Jeffrey C. Carrico is Acquisitions Librarian, Cline Library, Northern Arizona University (E-mail: jeff.carrico@nau.edu).

Kathleen L. Smalldon is Interim Associate University Librarian, Cline Library, Northern Arizona University (E-mail: Kathleen.Smalldon@nau.edu).

This article is based on a presentation given at the American Library Association's 2002 Summer Conference in Atlanta, GA, June 15, 2002.

[Haworth co-indexing entry note]: "Licensed to ILL: A Beginning Guide to Negotiating E-Resources Licenses to Permit Resource Sharing." Carrico, Jeffrey C., and Kathleen L. Smalldon. Co-published simultaneously in *Journal of Library Administration* (The Haworth Information Press, an imprint of The Haworth Press, Inc.) Vol. 40, No. 1/2, 2004, pp. 41-54; and: *The Changing Landscape for Electronic Resources: Content, Access, Delivery, and Legal Issues* (ed: Yem S. Fong, and Suzanne M. Ward) The Haworth Information Press, an imprint of The Haworth Press, Inc., 2004, pp. 41-54. Single or multiple copies of this article are available for a fee from The Haworth Document Delivery Service [1-800-HAWORTH, 9:00 a.m. - 5:00 p.m. (EST). E-mail address: docdelivery@haworthpress.com].

http://www.haworthpress.com/web/JLA
Digital Object Identifier: 10.1300/J111v40n01_04

KEYWORDS. Electronic resources, license agreements, interlibrary loan, resource sharing, document delivery

INTRODUCTION

This article introduces issues related to interlibrary loan and the electronic product licensing process to library staff involved with document delivery and interlibrary loan (ILL). Product licensing directly affects interlibrary loan services, but this fact is frequently lost in the complexities of the whole process. Armed with more information and a better understanding of licenses, however, the ILL librarian will become knowledgeable and comfortable enough with the process to contribute to the final outcome. Please note that issues concerning content, pricing, access, archiving, and the rest of the legalese involved with licensing are so numerous they are better served in other readings.

Electronic resources are more prolific than ever. Publishers move more and more information from print to electronic formats at an ever-increasing rate, requiring libraries to adapt to these new formats. As the format for materials changes from print to electronic, so do the users' needs and expectations change. Users expect and demand better, faster, and electronic access to all types of scholarship. Electronic resources may include, but are not limited to, full-text databases, online journals, technical reports, books, and dissertations. As a library's product list grows or changes, the number of required licenses grows with it. The rules were relatively simple with print resources where fair use and general ILL practice were standard operating procedure. With electronic resources, the playing field is far more complex. New publishers and products enter the field, each of them with their own license agreements. These agreements are very disparate in content and language. Today each license has its own set of somewhat negotiable "rules" that run the gamut of do's and don'ts, pricing, usage, user restrictions, access, penalties, and, invariably, resource sharing language.

Somehow in this mix, librarians are supposed to wade through all of the legal language and achieve a final contract that not only satisfies both the library and publisher, but also retains the rights to information use and sharing that libraries and users expect. It is to their credit that many libraries can and have managed to absorb these complex and daunting tasks so well.

Licenses are legal documents and as such they can be a miasma of legal language. Because of the complexity of the legal processes involved with licensing, many libraries appoint someone with legal experience, such as a lawyer, purchasing agent, or some other legal counsel, to serve as the primary negotiator for licensing material acquisitions. Commonly, this person does not work in a library and is not conversant with library issues and therefore has a steep learning curve about the access needs of library users. Complicating the issue, the publisher or vendor also often has legal counsel with little experience or understanding of how libraries and their patrons use the product. In our experience, this scenario is unfortunately the usual case, rather than the exception to the rule.

There is little doubt that in the past acquiring print materials involved fewer staff, time, energy, resources, and paper. Library negotiators and lawyers did not need to involve themselves in the traditional acquisitions process because license agreements, at least as we experience them today, did not exist. Print material was purchased and added to the physical collections with little thought about how that material would be used and accessed. ILL departments could easily search a library catalog to locate an item in the collection, retrieve it, copy it if required, and mail it to another library.

The players in the licensing negotiation process, particularly regarding ILL privileges, include the primary negotiator, the acquisitions librarian, and the ILL librarian or practitioner. It is critical that interlibrary loan librarians or practitioners identify the person at their institution who negotiates the licenses for electronic resources. As print materials become electronic, there is a greater risk that a library may lose its ability to lend or borrow needed research items through interlibrary loan because of a single clause in a license agreement. To protect services, the acquisition librarian should work closely with ILL staff to clarify the needs of the unit and its users.

Finally, the article identifies some ways that staff who are not directly involved in the licensing process can help heighten the awareness of the negotiators on both sides of the deal to consider including better and more useful resource sharing language in the contract.

DISCUSSION

In the last ten years, licensing issues have progressed from a small puzzling annoyance, such as the shrink-wrap licenses on some CD ROMs and videos, to a huge time- and resource-consuming process. Publishers increasingly move materials into electronic formats and, as libraries expand their electronic collections, the time spent on the initial acquisition of the products mushrooms. Small journals that were easy to acquire in their print format now potentially have pages of legal documents assigned to their acquisition. ILL language, good or bad, is usually part of every license agreement, but if it is not present a whole different set of problems arises.

ILL language in a license can potentially be quite restricting to the library. As electronic materials are substituted for print ones, librarians often discover that an item that they formerly lent in its print form may be prohibited from resource sharing in its electronic format. Librarians further discover that when their organization's negotiator reviewed and signed the licensing agreement, so much attention was concentrated on price, coverage, access, and other legal issues that little attention was paid to ILL language. Negotiators did not consider ILL as a priority due to a lack of awareness or because the library still had access to a print copy. Later, when the library phased out the print copy for the electronic, suddenly the rules changed and the content may not be shared with other libraries.

LICENSING SOLUTIONS
AT NORTHERN ARIZONA UNIVERSITY

At Northern Arizona University (NAU) in Flagstaff, ILL is part of the collection development plan. The institution is a medium-sized, undergraduate university with almost twenty thousand full- and part-time students engaged in pursuing almost two hundred different undergraduate and graduate degrees. There are more than eight hundred full- and part-time faculty in eleven colleges. Almost a third of these students are located away from the Flagstaff campus and do not have direct access to library materials except those offered online. Because of the large and diverse user population, as well as the increasingly expanding population of users off campus, the library has increased its electronic holdings dramatically and therefore its licensing responsibilities. In addition, the group of users is so disparate in its mix that the library's collection cannot meet everyone's needs as well as it would like. Recent budget constraints have intensified the problem, so interlibrary loan has become a critical part of the collection strategy. As ILL plays a greater role in the collection and as electronic holdings increase, the issue of ILL language in license agreements has become critical.

The acquisitions librarian at Northern Arizona University serves as the sole negotiator for all electronic resources, but this was not always the case. At first, the campus purchasing agent handled licensing agreements like any other purchasing legality. As the process for negotiating licenses became more complex, the library's budget director and several people in the Library took on the responsibility, until it finally settled with the acquisitions librarian. In the beginning, ILL language issues were dealt with like all the other issues in a license agreement and, fortunately, the library had a voice in the language of the contract, although it did not directly deal with the publishers. When the licensing negotiation duties transferred to the library itself, attention to all facets of the license increased. With the onset of additional electronic products and an increasing number of newcomers to the electronic publishing arena, the language in the contracts became more difficult to negotiate. The old guard in the publishing world was aware of ILL and incorporated it into their license agreements; however, the newer publishers often overlooked it or made it so restrictive that it was impossible to use the product for ILL at all. These publishers were understandably conservative in their approach to licenses, wanting to protect their products from being electronically shared without any safeguards. Unfortunately, their extreme concerns about access made the library's job of negotiating ILL permissions almost impossible.

As a result of the changing technology in document delivery and the larger, more complex acquisition deals that involved NAU, new negotiation procedures had to be established. Using model licenses and what librarians considered suitable language from some of the contracts already negotiated, staff created a section of ideal ILL language to use as a benchmark. Librarians also determined which ILL restrictions would not, under any circumstances, be included in the contracts and which restrictions were not worth contesting. Working with the ILL librarian, the acquisitions librarian attempts to negotiate better ILL language in all of NAU's electronic product contracts.

LICENSING GUIDELINES FOR LIBRARIANS

There are many things that a librarian can do to facilitate licensing agreements that permit resource sharing. Start by becoming educated in the area of license agreements. There are several online courses available through the American Library Association (ALA), the Association for Research Libraries (ARL), the Association of College and Research Libraries (ACRL), and other organizations. There are also many other licensing resources such as lists and websites; a selected list appears at the end of this article. An ILL librarian or practitioner does not need to be an expert, but a little knowledge certainly helps with understanding what is going on in the world of licensing.

Find the library's negotiator. It may sound simplistic, but the first step for an ILL librarian, practitioner, or anyone with an interest in the license negotiation process is finding out who actually conducts the negotiation. At first glance, it may seem obvious who is performing this task, but the person who you think handles the license agreements may only be the library contact associated with license agreements. In actual fact, a legal representative, purchasing agent, or another negotiator at a different institution, who is not even located in the library, is handling the real negotiation, as is often the case in a consortial license agreement. Their interests may be to complete the license legally, following all of the laws and rules applicable at the institution, but they may not be aware of the library's specific needs.

After identifying the true negotiator, let them know how the licensing language affects ILL's mission. Explain which ILL requirements are critical for an online product. Find out how long the library will have access to a particular resource and follow up with other issues such as format type or the availability of, access to, and length of, archives.

Actively take on the role of educator and advocate for ILL provisions. Consortial purchases may entail multiple levels of negotiators, with the actual people handling the language issues several levels away from the library. The consortium's interests, as a whole, are often the same as an individual library's interests, but the majority of the negotiator's time may be spent addressing several libraries' interests while crafting a document that pleases the publisher or vendor. Not every organization involved in the deal may have the same desires when it comes to ILL provisions. Work cooperatively with the negotiator to make sure all ILL contractual language is reviewed before the deal is finalized.

Identify "ideal" language for the library using model licenses, what was learned from previous licenses your library has been involved with, and what you consider the ideal ILL situation. It is possible to enter negotiations with a publisher who has little or no understanding of ILL and, therefore, no provisions in its contract concerning ILL. When approached on the subject, publishers are occasionally willing to consider what libraries offer as language for the transaction. If the original language is too restrictive, be prepared to offer the publisher alternative wording.

At NAU, the license negotiator (the acquisitions librarian) sends a copy of any ILL language to the ILL librarian for review. The ILL librarian marks up the copy of the language and the acquisitions librarian incorporates these changes into the collective comments sent to the publisher. Having educated the negotiator, it is then time to use diplomacy and begin the next stage of the ILL education process, educating the publisher. The publisher responds to the various requests submitted and, if needed, makes changes to the license. Ideally the licensing language should be clear and self-explanatory, but this is not often the case. It is not unusual for the negotiator to provide explanations to the publisher (or to request explanations from the publisher) about certain language that the negotiator wants to include in the license. These exchanges provide another opportunity to educate the publisher on the realities of interlibrary loan services. Occasionally, a license will contain language that appears restrictive concerning the sharing of articles with other users or institutions. However, when the language is discussed among the negotiating parties, it may become clear that the intention of the language is to restrict access only to for-profit entities or to document delivery services, not to "traditional" libraries. If the ILL language included in the license meets the library's minimum requirements and all parties are satisfied with the rest of the contract, the deal is struck.

EXAMPLES OF RESOURCE SHARING LICENSING LANGUAGE

Here are some examples of ILL licensing language ranging from a level that NAU librarians consider unacceptable language to ideal language.

Example A: Unacceptable Terms (Later Modified)

In this example, the license applies only to journals published by "<deleted>." Other publishers may have different conditions or may not permit interlibrary loan. NAU librarians felt that tracking the borrowing requests, collecting data, and sending a report to the publisher every six months were too extreme. This language was later deleted from the license.

> The Licensor grants Subscriber the right to use journal articles from those Licensed Products from "_____" that contain journal content (the "ILL Material") as source material for interlibrary loans on an article-by-article basis and under the following conditions, subject to exceptions for any publications and material noted below:

- the request comes from an academic or other non-commercial, non-corporate research library located in the same country as Subscriber; and "_____"
- the requested article is printed by Subscriber and mailed or faxed to the requesting library; and
- Subscriber refrains from advertising its interlibrary loan capability with respect to the ILL Material, or from otherwise advertising or soliciting interlibrary loan requests; and
- Subscriber delivers to the Licensor every six months a report covering the preceding six months which will identify the journals from which articles were providing during the relevant period (including publication year of such material) and the number of articles sent from each of said journal years . . .

Example B: Minimally Acceptable Terms

This license permits ILL, but staff have to print the article and then fax or mail it to the recipient, rather than taking advantage of electronic delivery methods, such as Ariel.

> The Licensee's library staff may print out and send by fax or mail single paper copies of articles from the Licensed Electronic Journals for interlibrary loan.

Example C: Better ILL Terms

The license permits Ariel or Prospero transmission, but NAU still cannot send a copy of the electronic file, no matter how secure the server is.

> The electronic form of the Licensed Materials may be used as a source for Interlibrary Loan whereby articles can be printed and these print copies be delivered via postal mail, fax, or fax-based services (e.g., Ariel or Prospero) to fulfill ILL requests from an academic, research or other non-commercial library. Requests received from for-profit companies or directly from individuals may not be honored. Direct digital transmission of files is not permitted.

Example D: Best ILL Terms

Although this example shows the best language obtained so far, it is still not perfect. However, the option of using a secure server to store the material for printing by the user is beneficial.

Supply to an Authorized User of another library (whether by post, fax or secure electronic transmission, using Ariel or its equivalent, whereby the electronic file is deleted immediately after printing), for the purposes of research or private study, a single paper copy of an electronic original of an individual document.

NEGOTIATING LICENSES

Invariably, there will come a time when no matter how many discussions and explanations have taken place, and when no matter how diplomatic and flexible the negotiator has been, there is still language in the license that the library feels is not acceptable. This is the time to walk away from the deal. NAU has declined to finalize several deals for good products because of issues for which there was no satisfactory resolution; the publishers' required "rules" were not right for the library's users. NAU has never yet backed out of a deal because of ILL language, but the library has stopped negotiations because of issues related to geographic restrictions and technology issues, such as proprietary plug-ins or user interfaces. These are always tough calls and it is up to the institution and the negotiator to determine where the line is drawn. Communicate these decisions to the vendor, so they know why the deal has fallen through. This step will help educate them as to what terms libraries are willing to accept or not accept when it comes to products and licenses.

On the whole, publishers recognize that in the library world ILL is an integrated service. Although publishers usually try to be accommodating, the NAU experience has been that they want to keep the mechanisms of ILL as procedural and complicated as possible. This complexity offers them more checks and balances in the system to serve as safeguards that protect the publishers' considerable investment in the products' content.

It is still very common to see ILL language in a contract that requires printing an electronic document or article, and then faxing the item to the recipient library that, in turn, passes it on to the end user. Fortunately more licenses now permit Ariel; hopefully it will soon be common to see language that allows the unmediated transfer of electronic documents from the lender to a server where the recipients may access the documents on their desktops.

Model licenses dot the landscape and many of them have some good ideas that should be incorporated into any ideal license. Janet Croft refers to a number of model licenses (Croft, 2001). However, model licenses are just that–models–and may need to be modified for a particular institution. Unfortunately, most publishers do not use a model license when drafting their own license, thus negating the model license idea, so it is important to know what provisions or language the library will accept completely, accept grudgingly, or absolutely not accept. At NAU, permission to provide interlibrary loan service is one of those items that is a potential deal-breaker.

Strong negotiation educates both the negotiator and the vendor and results in the successful acquisition of electronic products. It is through the act of negotiation that the ILL process can be strengthened to meet the needs of the users. As more libraries champion the cause and request less restrictive ILL permissions, more publishers will hear the message. As more publishers modify their agreements to ease the restrictions around ILL, the others will see that it can be accomplished without the loss of content or the danger of unrestricted access.

As stated previously, communication is important between the library's license negotiator and the ILL department. This simple process of communicating about proposed ILL language can help define use of electronic resources internally to the institution and also defend the rights of all ILL units to serve other libraries. In some situations it may be necessary to indicate that a library is willing to walk away from the purchase of a resource if necessary. If the vendor or publisher is unwilling to be flexible with its license and permit even limited ILL use of materials, it may not be worth the purchase price. As development of electronic resources continues, "online" may soon become the only purchasing option. This significant change in format makes it critical for libraries to retain the rights associated with resource sharing.

Tracking all of the different "ILL rules" for a particular online resource can be overwhelming. Depending on how well a license is negotiated, the experience of using online resources for ILL may be fairly straightforward or as daunting as reaching the top of Mt. Everest. At NAU, Document Delivery Services keeps the process as simple as possible. By coordinating with the acquisitions librarian, ILL staff obtain copies of the ILL sections within the different product licenses. The NAU library currently subscribes to more than 130 online databases; however, ILL only fills requests from approximately eight databases. The reason for limiting the number of databases that ILL uses to fill requests is the consistency of the licenses' "rules," methods for delivery, and the number of requests historically filled from a particular database. Document Delivery Services employees search a lending request in the library catalog and determine if it is in print or electronic format. In many cases, the catalog links directly to the electronic title in a particular database. Staff review the short list of databases that permit ILL. If the database is listed, staff print the article for delivery via mail, fax, or even Ariel. NAU ILL currently fills only five percent of lending requests from electronic resources. This percentage will increase over time as libraries switch to all-electronic formats. The perception within the ILL community is that libraries will not fill requests from online resources because of restrictive language in the license agreements. In many cases this is true because libraries are not negotiating more flexible lending terms for their ILL offices. Another contributing factor to the low use of online databases for ILL is that there are separate bibliographic records for print and electronic titles. Generally, staff will not order materials from other libraries using a bibliographic record for an online title, but focus only on the print records. As collections evolve and change from print to electronic, this perception should fade. The separation of the print and electronic bibliographic records will begin to blur as collections convert from one format to another.

One may ask: is ILL a privilege or a right? As budgets remain flat or decline, ILL is no longer only a privilege, but a vital means of providing access to materials that cannot be added to a collection. Since the pace of scholarly publishing far outstrips today's libraries' resources for acquiring all the material that might be desirable, ILL becomes a right for users.

CONCLUSION

In the library world, electronic products seem to be taking over, especially when it comes to serials. New products and publishers mean new license agreements and a lot of time spent dealing with them. In this ever changing scenario, interlibrary loan users' needs are more important than ever. While each ILL librarian has a local role to play in license negotiation, the collective voice of all ILL librarians can change publishers' perceptions of interlibrary loan needs for all institutions.

Fulfilling the ILL librarian's role in license negotiations includes the following:

- Identify the actual negotiator for library electronic products.
- Draft ideal resource sharing language. Determine what points that the library is willing or not willing to accept as language from publishers.

- Be diplomatic and help educate not only the institution's license negotiator, but also the publishers.
- Concentrate on obtaining the best ILL terms for the resources that are most heavily used in resource sharing, rather than focusing on every electronic resource that might potentially fill ILL requests.
- Learn what terms can be negotiated, such as requirements that the institution track how many times articles are printed for ILL use.
- Be prepared to walk away from a deal that does not satisfy the library's minimum requirements.

Most libraries that lend materials through interlibrary loan already incorporate different formats into the retrieval process. Locating articles in full-text databases is no more complicated than retrieving a video from the media collection. Schedule the full-text retrieval to be done once or twice a day to meet established turnaround times. Keep a short list of databases that permit ILL lending and make note of any delivery restrictions. For example, a license might prohibit Ariel delivery, but allow faxing. Obviously, the most efficient way to deliver articles is electronically, so fight for the right to deliver articles using Ariel or a similar electronic delivery mechanism.

Using a database to store and retrieve ILL information concerning electronic materials is helpful. At NAU, staff created an in-house database for ILL purposes, but are evaluating other, more robust information systems to hold not only data concerning ILL, but other electronic product information. TDNet is an example of a commercial product that meets these multiple needs.

ILL librarians look forward to the time when electronic product licenses become more homogenous, when publishers relax their restrictions, and when the technology advances to allow transmission of ILL documents directly to users' desktops. As a library accumulates electronic materials, it is the ILL librarian's duty to make sure that current needs are being met while staying alert to meet future needs.

NOTES

Bebbington, Laurence. 2001. "Managing Content: Licensing, Copyright, and Privacy issues in Managing Electronic Resources." *Legal Information Management* 1(2):4-12.

Brennan, Patricia, Karen Hersey, and Georgia Harper. (1997) "Strategic and Practical Considerations for Signing Electronic Information Delivery Agreements." <http://arl.cni.org/scomm/licensing/licbooklet.html> (June 3, 2002).

Croft, Janet Brennan. 2001. "Model Licences and Interlibrary Loan/Document Delivery from Electronic Resources." *Interlending & Document Supply* 29(4): 165-8.

Pike, George H. 2001. "A Book Is a Book Is an E-Book: Copyright, Contract, and Technology Are Clashing in the Digital Age." *Information Today* 18(7): 19-21.

Thompson, Laurie and Sandhya D. Srivastava. (2002). "Licensing Electronic Resources." *Serials Librarian* 42(1/2):7-12.

RESOURCES

Listservs

Liblicense-L

A moderated list that deals with licensing issues. If you follow only one list about licensing issues, this is the one.
http://www.library.yale.edu/~llicense/ListArchives/

ARL E-Journal Forum

List for all facets of e-journal management, including licensing.
http://www.cni.org/Hforums/arl-ejournal/

Acqnet

List for all things related to acquisitions. Some electronic media and licensing issues occasionally come up.
http://acqweb.library.vanderbilt.edu/acqweb/acqnet.html

Digital Copyright

List for all things (and all people) dealing with digital copyright issues.
http://www.umuc.edu/distance/odell/cip/listserv.html

ERIL

Electronic Resources in Libraries.
http://listserv.binghamton.edu/archives/eril-l.html

Internet

Berkeley Digital Library, *Copyright, Intellectual Property Rights, and Licensing Issues* 1 March 2002.
http://sunsite.berkeley.edu/Copyright/ (3 June 2002).

Catchword, LTD. *LicensingModels.Com.*
http://www.licensingmodels.com/ (3 June 2002).

International Federation of Library Associations and Institutions. *Licensing Principles (2001)*. 1 May 2001.
http://www.ifla.org/V/ebpb/copy.htm (3 June 2002).

Yale University Library. *LibLicense: Licensing Digital Information.* 11 June 2002.
http://www.library.yale.edu/~llicense/index.shtml. (12 December 2002).

North Carolina State University Libraries. *Scholarly Communication Center.* 7 February 2002.
http://www.lib.ncsu.edu/scc/licensing/licensing.html. (12 December 2002).

Open Source Software
and Resource Sharing

Jeff A. Steely

SUMMARY. This article describes the open source software movement as a form of resource sharing and examines the possible benefits of using open source products in resource sharing operations. A sample of open source applications designed for resource sharing is supplemented by a list of several other applications that may interest resource sharing librarians. Readers can then imagine what a "gourmet" resource sharing system might look like. The article also suggests some possible steps for developing such a system. *[Article copies available for a fee from The Haworth Document Delivery Service: 1-800-HAWORTH. E-mail address: <docdelivery@haworth press.com> Website: <http://www.HaworthPress.com> © 2004 by The Haworth Press, Inc. All rights reserved.]*

KEYWORDS. Open source, software, resource sharing, interlibrary loan

INTRODUCTION: SHARING RECIPES

At a charity bake sale, you notice two loaves of bread. One loaf has the recipe attached, the other does not. Which loaf are you most likely to buy, the Recipe Bread or the Mystery Loaf? If you have food allergies

---

Jeff A. Steely is Assistant Director for Client Services, Baylor University Libraries (E-mail: Jeffrey_Steely@baylor.edu).

[Haworth co-indexing entry note]: "Open Source Software and Resource Sharing." Steely, Jeff A. Co-published simultaneously in *Journal of Library Administration* (The Haworth Information Press, an imprint of The Haworth Press, Inc.) Vol. 40, No. 1/2, 2004, pp. 55-69; and: *The Changing Landscape for Electronic Resources: Content, Access, Delivery, and Legal Issues* (ed: Yem S. Fong, and Suzanne M. Ward) The Haworth Information Press, an imprint of The Haworth Press, Inc., 2004, pp. 55-69. Single or multiple copies of this article are available for a fee from The Haworth Document Delivery Service [1-800-HAWORTH, 9:00 a.m. - 5:00 p.m. (EST). E-mail address: docdelivery@haworthpress.com].

http://www.haworthpress.com/web/JLA
© 2004 by The Haworth Press, Inc. All rights reserved.
Digital Object Identifier: 10.1300/J111v40n01_05

55

or are on a special diet, the recipe lets you determine whether the loaf is one you can eat. The Mystery Loaf could make you sick (or thick!). If you choose the Recipe Bread and like it, you can make a loaf yourself, experiment with the recipe, and even improve the final product. The Mystery Loaf, by contrast, would be a one-time experience. You can't improve upon the original, and you may never be able to have that type of bread again.

Now imagine yourself at a library conference. Several vendors offer competing resource sharing management systems. They do not share the "recipe" for their software. You can not view the source code–this is closed source software. Each vendor wants you to purchase its Mystery Module. The sales people extol the virtues of their respective products and promise an extensive list of planned enhancements, but none will tell you how the software works. After your visit to the exhibit hall, you walk to the auditorium for a presentation. Several librarians tell the audience about the resource sharing software that they have developed and will share at no cost. They have an e-mail list for users to discuss the software, and they will share the "recipe"–this is open source software (OSS). While the module does not have all of the features you would like, some of these desired features are under development at other libraries and, because you are technically inclined, you can work on the source code to create the additional features yourself. Which software would you choose?

After a brief discussion of open source software and its relationship to librarianship and resource sharing, this article will list some of the current items on the OSS resource sharing "menu." While there are only a handful of OSS programs specifically designed for resource sharing, this first ingredient in the recipe will be supplemented by a list of several other applications that may interest resource sharing librarians. Readers will then have the opportunity to imagine what a "gourmet" resource sharing system might look like. The article concludes by suggesting some possible next steps for cooking up such a system.

OPEN SOURCE SOFTWARE

Computer programs are written in readable programming languages like C++ or Java. A programmer can read this "source code" and understand how the program works. The computer, however, does not run the source code. The program must be compiled into machine language, a string of 1's and 0's, that the computer can understand.[1] This binary machine code is, for all intents and purposes, unintelligible to humans, and therefore disguises the inner workings of the program. When one buys (or, more typically, licenses) computer software, the purchaser usually just gets the compiled binaries, and not the source code. The user program is then completely dependent on the vendor for bug fixes, enhancements, and support. This is a "closed source" model.

Open source software distribution allows the end user to see the source code. Open source license agreements allow the user to modify and share the code as well. The only real restriction on use is that the OSS cannot be incorporated into a closed source product. The power of OSS, particularly in a highly networked world, is that many programmers can collaborate to improve the code, and then share the new and improved "recipe."[2]

LIBRARIANSHIP AND OPEN SOURCE

Open source seems like a recipe for chaos. The open source community, however, has developed a culture that regulates the development of open source projects with a high degree of efficiency. Required reading on this topic is Eric S. Raymond's collection of essays, *The Cathedral and the Bazaar*, an anthropological study of the hacker culture.[3] One especially interesting aspect of Raymond's analysis is the explanation of hacker norms as a "gift culture." In a society with an abundance of resources, status is achieved by what one gives away. For hackers with access to everything they need to program, status equates to reputation among peers. One of the best ways to enhance one's reputation is to give away the code one writes.[4]

Eric Lease Morgan (Head, Digital Access and Information Architecture, University Libraries of Notre Dame) points out that libraries, too, are concerned about reputation, and, like open source developers, "gain reputation by the amount of 'stuff' they give away."[5] Daniel Chudnov (developer of jake and maintainer of the OSS4LIB website/e-mail list), another leading advocate of OSS development in libraries, has also pointed to the similarities in the cultures, comparing the relationship between libraries and their clients with that of OSS and the software industry.[6] Art Rhyno, also active in the development of open source library tools, believes that a library open source development may need to occur in a "community that is predisposed towards resource-sharing."[7] This parallel between the cultures is interesting, but does it have any practical meaning?

A group of library administrators thinks so. In September 1999, participants in the ARL/OCLC Strategic Issues Forum for Academic Library Directors drafted the "Keystone Principles."[8] They developed these principles "to guide academic libraries' efforts and establish a foundation for joint future-oriented action based on traditional academic library values."[9] The affinity between OSS and libraries is evident in the second of the four Keystone Principles: "Libraries are responsible for creating innovative information systems for the dissemination and preservation of information and new knowledge regardless of format."[10] The action steps under this principle suggest that libraries should redirect some money from traditional budget lines to support cooperative development of these new systems. The action steps also include expectations that these systems will be unbiased and based on librarian knowledge of customer needs. Additionally, and most relevant to the comparison between OSS and librarianship, is the action step that calls for libraries to "create interoperability in the systems they develop and create open source software for the access, dissemination, and management of information."[11] This coupling of forward-looking librarianship with library-developed open source systems is a new section in the library "cookbook." Who, then, will submit the recipes?

There are some good "recipes" out there. Yet if one compares the ratio of closed source to open source systems in a typical library, it is clear that most libraries still prefer to "eat out." Where is "home cooking" (open source development) most likely to happen? Morgan points out that "libraries have spent a lot of time, effort, and money on resource sharing."[12] He then asks, "Why not pool these same resources together to create software that will satisfy our professional needs?"[13] While this could, at first glance, seem like a threat to resource sharing ("He wants to move our funding to the IT folks?!?"), Morgan's question merely suggests that resource sharing has set a precedent of cooperation. Morgan even refers to OSS as a form of "resource sharing."[14] Resource sharing librarians and staff, currently at the forefront of the cooperative efforts between libraries, seem logical advocates for this new form of resource sharing, OSS development. Perhaps, then, resource sharing applications could be among the first recipes to come out of the test kitchen.

There are, in fact, several OSS applications currently available that were designed for resource sharing, and at least one group is working on a complete open source resource sharing management system. Other current OSS applications that are not specifically for resource sharing are potential sources for useful code or as partner applications to resource sharing systems.[15] All of these projects may contribute ingredients to an open source, gourmet resource sharing system (GRSS) in the future.

CURRENT OSS FOR RESOURCE SHARING

Perhaps the most familiar OSS application in resource sharing circles is Prospero, the document delivery software developed at Ohio State University's Prior Health Sciences Library (available at http://bones.med.ohio-state.edu/index.htm). Originally an Ariel® add-on to allow electronic document delivery to end users, Prospero now includes scanning capabilities. Prospero can, therefore, serve as an open source alternative to Ariel.

Any resource sharing librarian is aware of the many demands on staff at the supplying (lending) library. ILL ASAP (automatic search and print) was developed by Kyle Banerjee at Oregon State University to automate several time-consuming and error-prone processes in ILL lending. ILL ASAP is a Visual Basic Script that parses a plain text file of OCLC requests, downloaded using OCLC's MicroEnhancer, and extracts data from each request. This data is used to search an Innovative Interfaces, Inc. Web OPAC. After searching the OPAC and grabbing location, holdings, and status information, the program creates an XML file that combines the data points from the requests and the OPAC. Finally, ILL ASAP prints pick slips that include the original request; location, holdings, and availability information extracted from the OPAC, and also barcodes to facilitate checkout and delivery. Baylor University's Interlibrary Services office has modified ILL ASAP version 1.1 for local use, adding mailing labels, additional barcodes, the university's logo, and some business rule logic to determine shipping method preferences.[16] These changes would have been impossible with closed source software. An enhanced and easier to install version 2.x of the program, written in PowerBasic and designed by Banerjee and Terry Reese, is now available at <http://www.onid.orst.edu/~reeset/illasap/>.

Olivet Nazarene University has shared several OSS recipes. One current offering is an ISO-compliant ILL Web form, ILL Wizard 1.0, which allows patrons to submit ILL requests directly to OCLC's Direct Request. Olivet also offers several OCLC Passport macros written by Joe Gutekanst of Davidson College Library. Two of these macros automate part of the ILL lending process of searching for holdings and replying to requesting libraries. Another macro parses a borrowing request that is received as a formatted e-mail message, and then enters the extracted data into an OCLC workform. All of these items are available at <http://library.olivet.edu/opensource/opensource.html>.

Crawford County Federated Library System (CCFLS) in Pennsylvania has an ILL component as part of their union catalog. Users are offered an ILL button when viewing a bibliographic record in the catalog. This button launches an authorization window that requests a user name and password. Only librarians are able to use the feature. Once the librarian is authenticated, the system presents a web form. The script automatically places bibliographic information for the title being requested into the form, and retrieves information identifying the requesting librarian and his/her library from a cookie. This e-mail is then ready to go to the library in the system that owns the item.[17]

OTHER OSS PROJECTS OF INTEREST

In the title essay of Raymond's *The Cathedral and the Bazaar*, the author lists principles for effective development of open source systems. The second principle is: "Good programmers know what to write. Great ones know what to rewrite and reuse."[18] A wonderful thing about open source software is that it is possible, and legally permissible, to rewrite and reuse code. The resource sharing applications mentioned above all have obvious, immediate application for the practitioner. Some less obvious choices may provide ingredients for future, open source resource sharing systems.

The many open source course reserve programs that are available represent one such pool of potentially useful code. The list of electronic reserve applications includes:

- course/control, developed at Emory University, available at: http://coursecontrol.sourceforge.net/
- FreeReserves, developed by programmers at the University of Southern Illinois, Carbondale, and Augsburg College, available at: http://www.lib.umn.edu/san/freereserves/
- UKReserves (version of FreeReserves), developed at City University, London, available at: http://vlib.city.ac.uk/code/
- OSCR (Open Source Course Reserve), developed at George Mason University, available at: http://lso.gmu.edu/OSCR/
- Web Access Reserve Program (WARP), developed at Olivet Nazarene University, available at: http://library.olivet.edu/warp.html.

While serving a different library function, these systems share some similarities with Prospero. Many of the component processes, such as scanning, document management, user authentication, and web delivery are similar. Though these e-reserve packages may not be of immediate interest to ILL practitioners, some of the code may be useful for assembling a GRSS.

Search interface and linking tools may also contain useful source code for the GRSS. Librarians want to make things simpler for their clients. Research would be much simpler if clients were able to identify what they need from one search interface that can query both Z39.50 and non-Z39.50 databases. Several commercial, closed source products provide such a service, but open source tools are also available. One example is OCLC's SiteSearch (available at http://www.sitesearch.oclc.org/helpzone/main.html). Another cross-database search interface, dbWiz (information is available at http://www.lib.sfu.ca/dbwiz/), is under development at Simon Fraser University (SFU) for COPPUL (Council of Prairie and Pacific University Libraries). A third option for the technologically ambitious is building a new client from open source tools, such as JZKit (http://developer.k-int.com/products/jzkit/) or YAZ (http://www.index data.dk/yaz/).

Once a client discovers potentially useful resources, linking software can make it easier to (1) discover where the resource resides; (2) get/request the item; and/or (3) find related resources. The GODOT Holdings/Requesting/Fulltext Module (information at http://godot.lib.sfu.ca/), another COPPUL project, is a good example of such software. COPPUL is in the process of redesigning the software, but the existing version provides many of the features of closed source, OpenURL-based programs. OpenURL provides a standard way of moving data from one place to another. One pertinent application of this standard for resource sharing is the migration of citation data from citation databases to resource sharing request forms. The improved quality and completeness of the data on request forms can make it easier to fill requests, perhaps even allowing a resource sharing module to process the request automatically.

Another library open source project is jake (jointly administered knowledge environment, available at http://jake-db.org/). Jake, which was developed under the direction of Daniel Chudnov at the Cushing/Whitney Medical Library at the Yale University School of Medicine, is a database that maps journal titles to electronic indexes and full-text databases. Simon Fraser University has taken on a lead role in maintaining and developing jake with their installation of the system (http://jake.lib.sfu.ca/). SFU is motivated in part by the fact that the COPPUL GODOT system uses the SFUjake data to provide its linking service. Jake, like the other OSS pieces above, may be a useful ingredient for a GRSS.

One should not think about developing or purchasing a library module like a resource sharing management system without at least considering how that system might interact with the library's integrated library system (ILS). A GRSS could, for example, share the ILS patron database for authentication, and could interact with the circulation module of the ILS to create records for circulating ILL materials. An open source ILS would allow developers to get "under the hood" of the ILS and streamline movement of data between the ILS and the GRSS. Most libraries, however, use a proprietary, closed source ILS. Creating an entire ILS with an open source model is difficult due to the size and complexity of the task relative to the number of library programmers available. Part of the phenomenal success of the open source Linux operating system was the pool of developers with the ability and desire to work on development. This "bazaar" model described so well by Raymond may not scale down to the much smaller collection of library-based programmers.[19] In contrast to the thousands of developers who might jump onto a newly released Linux snippet to search for bugs or ways to improve the code, it seems likely that a just handful of librarians would dive into the code of an open source ILS. Nevertheless there are several open source ILS projects underway.

Koha, developed by Katipo Communications Ltd. for the Horowhenua Library Trust of New Zealand, is a production system with catalogue, OPAC, circulation, and acquisitions components. Other open source ILS projects include the LearningAccess ILS (http://www.learningaccess. org/website/techdev/ils.php); OpenOPAC from Facultad de Ciencias Exactas y Naturales de la Universidad de Buenos Aires (FCEN-UBA) and the Biblioteca Central "Dr. Luis F. Leloir" of FCEN-UBA (Central Library) (http://www.bl.fcen.uba.ar/openopac.php); OpenBiblio (http://obiblio.sourceforge.net/); and PhpMyLibrary (http://phpmy library.sourceforge.net/) designed by Polerio Babao Jr. II. Avanti MicroLCS is another OSS ILS slated for release in January 2003 according to project manager Peter Schlumpf.

The very concept of the ILS may get in the way of open source progress. Librarians have grown accustomed to depending upon a big-ticket, proprietary, closed source ILS. Another model to consider is a structure in which, as Morgan suggests, "existing open source software can be glued together . . . resulting in a sum greater than its parts."[20] Standards can hold this kind of structure together, but, as Art Rhyno points out, there needs to be general agreement on the overall "architectural layout" in order to "to allow all hands to contribute to its success."[21] Rhyno has been developing his Pytheas system (http://venus.uwindsor.ca/library/leddy/people/art/pytheas/index.html) under this model. One part that could be "glued" to this structure is an open source GRSS. The complicated GRSS could, in turn, be tackled piece by piece in an open source environment.

IMAGINING THE OSS
GOURMET RESOURCE SHARING SYSTEM

What might the GRSS look like? What are the features you would like to see? Imagine this scenario: Your library's client searches multiple databases simultaneously using SiteSearch. When browsing through a sorted hit list, many items of interest are available full text and the client quickly and easily links to the full text through an open source OpenURL resolver (GODOT?). Other items are only available from other libraries. For these items, the OpenURL resolver offers a link to an online request form. The bibliographic data from the original database is automatically transferred to the request form, so that the client only needs to enter a username and password to connect this new request to their existing client account in the GRSS (or, if using his/her personal computer, a cookie could provide the identification data). The GRSS then takes over. It automatically does a Z39.50 search of the catalogs of consortial partners. If the item is available from one of these partners, GRSS checks out the item in the partner library's circulation system using NCIP (NISO Circulation Interchange Protocol).[22] If the item is not available at a partner library, the system simultaneously checks OCLC's WorldCat, RLIN's Eureka, the British Library's catalog, and a list of other library catalogs for possible suppliers. For journal requests holdings data is also collected. Holdings data is compared with the request. Libraries that lack the issue required will be deleted from the list of possible suppliers. If GRSS is not confident that it can read the holdings information, or if a library has not added holdings to the union list, this data will be stored for human review, if such a review becomes necessary.

GRSS maintains a prioritized list of lenders. This list is based on average turnaround time for previous requests from that library, average time required for "cannot supply" updates, and any other statistics available from the GRSS database.[23] Costs, delivery methods, group membership, and location could also be used to help set these priorities, based on the data in the GRSS and/or the new, standards-based policies database hosted by OCLC.[24] GRSS compares this list of preferred lenders to the available suppliers for a given item and creates a string of potential lenders in order of preference, building in load leveling if required or desired. The request, still unmediated (unless no matches were found) is sent to the first potential supplier via the preferences set in the supplier's GRSS profile and/or based on a real-time query of the OCLC policies database. The status of the request will be kept current via ISO ILL protocols. If the request is not filled, GRSS will automatically send the request to the next lender in the string.

If GRSS is unable to find a match for the item requested, borrowing staff review the request. Suppose the client entered a request without any ISSN and used an abbreviated journal title. Once the journal title has been corrected, the staff member can, with one click, have GRSS check a customized, local jake database to determine whether electronic full text is available. If online full text is not an option, the GRSS will go through its normal, automated search process, or the staff member can use a set of tools to search quickly for potential sources.

How does the GRSS work at the supplying (lending) library? The request is received via ISO ILL. At preset intervals, batches of requests are processed by GRSS. GRSS queries the local catalog for holdings information, and can automatically answer "no" with appropriate reasons for items that will not be sent, based on the item status (e.g., checked out), item location (e.g., non-circulating), or item not held. The GRSS can also send a conditional message, if appropriate, based on data in the request itself (e.g., lack of copyright compliance, cost above limits). The system can also place these rejected requests into a file for lending staff review. GRSS prints pick slips, similar to those from ILL ASAP, that include barcodes for easy processing. These pick slips double as book straps. Each slip also includes a shipping label with the appropriate shipping method determined by the requesting library's profile in GRSS and/or their policy database entry. Items that are physically shipped are updated with the barcode on the pick slip and the book's barcode or radio frequency identification (RFID) tag. Articles, which are supplied electronically using Prospero, are updated with barcodes. Data from the borrowing library's request are included in the GEDI metadata shipped with the TIFF file.

The borrowing library updates its system when staff receive a book by scanning a barcode supplied on the book strap by the lending library. A return label is also included as part of the book strap. The process of scanning the book creates a temporary item record in the local circulation system, using NCIP protocol (so that the local client can check out the material. Electronic documents are automatically routed to the requestor based on the GEDI metadata, and the borrowing library's GRSS is automatically updated to "received." Canned email messages automatically notify clients of the status of their requests. The client is also able to manage requests through a real-time, web-based interface.

You, as the resource sharing librarian, are able to use a report writing feature that generates statistical summaries of all resource sharing activities. Your director is very pleased by your statistical report because it shows that your turnaround times have decreased while handling twice as many requests with the same number of staff.

BUILDING THE GRSS

What will it take to create such a fantastic, open source resource sharing system? COPPUL, mentioned above for their innovative GODOT and dbWiz projects, provides one model with their OpenILL initiative. Several COPPUL libraries are collaborating to build a resource sharing management system. Mark Leggot, University Librarian at the University of Winnipeg, launched the discussion of building an open source resource sharing system for COPPUL and is the project administrator for OpenILL. This program was scheduled for release to development partners in the first quarter of 2003.[25] OpenILL could be the gourmet system of the future, and the starting point for development by the entire resource sharing community. At the very least COPPUL's OpenILL project provides one model for OSS development in libraries–development through consortial cooperation.

Librarians can also cooperate on open source in less formal ways, following the "bazaar" model described by Raymond. Resource sharing librarians and staff with programming skills can take the initiative to work with existing open source tools. Those that have a "personal itch" for an open source resource sharing management system can begin piecing together some code.[26]

Library administrators and mangers can assist with the development of useful, open source tools like GRSS by allowing their staff to "scratch" those personal itches, whether that means getting out of the way and allowing the experts in the trenches to seek the best solutions, or perhaps even encouraging staff members to develop programming skills. This kind of professional development is a great way to add value to a department during those weeks of the year when resource sharing volume drops. Managers interested in open source can also look for people with advanced computer skills when hiring resource sharing employees.

Some programmers are obviously necessary for open source development, but non-programmers should not feel left out. They can fill important roles in the development of an open source GRSS. Chudnov lists testing and providing feedback on systems, writing documentation, and creating instructional materials as other important tasks for library staff in open source projects.[27] What about the vendors in the exhibit hall? What can they gain from open source, and how can they participate? If the vendors view themselves primarily as sellers of computer programs, they will have little incentive to open their source code. If, however, some vendors view their business as primarily one of software support, then perhaps they could imagine their place in an open source environment.

Finally, one must ask what role the historic big players in resource sharing, such as OCLC and RLG, could or should play in the development of an open source GRSS. These organizations have invested in resource sharing products and services that provide tremendous benefits for member and non-member libraries alike. Both have promoted resource sharing and worked for the development and implementation of standards. OCLC's Interlibrary Loan Subsystem is the largest resource sharing network in the world, and the organization has made an exciting move to support open source development.[28] RLG's Ariel has been the unofficial standard for electronic delivery of resources between libraries for years. Clearly both organizations understand that resource sharing is a vital part of the cooperation they all seek to support and enhance.

One can question, however, whether their roles as vendors sometimes conflict with these greater aims. Commitments to proprietary, closed source resource sharing management systems may prevent OCLC (with its OCLC ILLiad product) and RLG (which offers ILL Manager) from considering the significant link between the concept of resource sharing and the goals of open source software development. RLG's sale of Ariel to Infotrieve supports this disconnect, as the member-based non-profit sold the program to a for-profit document delivery firm that, from one perspective, competes with library resource sharing. The explanation given for the sale by James Michalko (RLG president and CEO), that Ariel is to a point that it "needs the added resources that a commercial vendor can provide,"[29] gives further evidence of a failure to see the link between resource sharing and OSS. Perhaps it will take an organization which is interested in resource sharing but not in the business of selling software, such as the Association of Research Libraries (ARL), to lead the way.

CONCLUDING THOUGHTS

The GRSS described above is not hard to imagine, in part because most of the ingredients are already in the pantry as open source packages: SiteSearch, Prospero, ILL ASAP, open source databases like MySQL or PostgreSQL, etc. Furthermore, standards are available to bind the ingredients together. Resource sharing librarians can choose to buy the closed source products that are currently available, and then depend upon their vendor's enhancement processes to add the additional features that libraries need. For those resource sharing hackers who are not satisfied with this type of dependency, however, it is time to get in the kitchen to whip up something new.

NOTES

1. For the sake of simplicity this article does not discuss the difference between compiled and interpreted programming languages. Any introductory programming text will provide an explanation of the difference.

2. This is a brief and simplified description of open source. For the authoritative Open Source Definition, visit <http://www.opensource.org/docs/definition.php>. There is a debate between "free software" and "open source" camps. The "free software" movement has a level of hostility toward commercial software that is not shared by most that would claim the "open source" label. For more information, see the Free Software Foundation's web site, <http://www.fsf.org>, and the Open Source Initiative's web site, <http://www.opensource.org>.

3. Raymond uses the term "hacker" differently in *The Cathedral and the Bazaar*, rev. ed. (Sebastopol, Calif.: O'Reilly, 2001) from how it has been used in popular media. Raymond attempts to reclaim the term "hacker" in its "true and original sense" as referring to "an enthusiast, an artist a tinkerer, a problem solver, an expert," (xii) not as someone who breaks into computer systems.

4. Raymond, "Homesteading the Noosphere," in *The Cathedral & the Bazaar*, 81.

5. Eric Lease Morgan comments on Raymond's "gift culture" analysis of the open source movement and its similarities with librarianship in "Gift Cultures, Librarianship, and Open Source Software Development," 1 January 2001, <http://www.infomotions.com/musings/gift-cultures.shtml> (2 January 2003).

6. Daniel Chudnov, "Open Source Software: The Future of Library Systems?" *Library Journal* 124, no.13 (August 1999): 41.

7. Art Rhyno, "Update," 30 April 2002, <http://listserv.arizona.edu/cgi-bin/wa?A2=ind0204&L=osdls&T=0&F=&S=&P=342> (2 January 2003).

8. The Association of Research Libraries, the ARL Office of Leadership and Management Services, and the Online Computer Library Center, "The Keystone Principles," 8 October 1999, <http://www.arl.org/training/keystone.html>, (30 December 2002).

9. Ibid.

10. Ibid.

11. Ibid.

12. Eric Morgan, "Possibilities for Open Source Software in Libraries," *Information Technology and Libraries* 21, no.1 (March 2002): 14-15.

13. Ibid., 14.

14. Ibid.

15. As projects come and go, this list will rapidly become obsolete. For the latest on open source software in libraries, visit the OSS4LIB website at <http://www.OSS4lib.org>.

16. Sample pick slips produced by Baylor's version of ILL ASAP can be viewed at <http://www3.baylor.edu/~Jeffrey_Steely/presentations/coill2002/asap_samples.doc>/.

17. A brief description of this capability was included in Richard Poynder, "The Open Source Movement: Does this software provide a viable, user-friendly alternative to proprietary solutions?" *Information Today* 18, no.9 (October 2001): 67. This information was supplemented by a phone call between the author and Cindy Murdock, Network Administrator, Meadville Public Library & Crawford County Federated Library System, on 7 January 2003.

18. Raymond, 24.

19. Art Rhyno credits Dan Chudnov with the observation that "it takes an urban population to support a bazaar and we may not have enough of a crowd to reach the levels described by Eric Raymond" in "Update," 30 April 2002.

20. Morgan, "OSSNLibraries-Open Source Software 'N Libraries," 11 June 2002 <http://www.infomotions.com/musings/ossnlibraries.shtml> (2 January 2003), Redefining the ILS.

21. Rhyno also points out in "ERP Options in an OSS World" 1 November 2002, <http://usrlib.info:28080/story/2002/10/31/10935/696> (12 January 2003) that not all of the pieces of such a system must, or even should, be written specifically for an ILS. He states that "it makes more sense to have developers who have a deep understanding of the underlying data models to craft the pieces of the system that reflect the processes the data model is designed for"–such as using software developed for the accounting world for acquisitions, as opposed to building the acquisitions module from the ground up.

22. Information on NCIP, also known as ANSI/NISO Z39.83-2002, is available at <http://www.niso.org/committees/committee_at.html>.

23. Baylor's Interlibrary Services unit is doing something like this with OCLC Management Statistics and "Reasons for No" statistics. They use a homemade Microsoft Access (sorry, free software zealots!) database to create their OCLC custom holdings lists. Potential suppliers are grouped based on charges, average turnaround time, percentage of requests that "age" (move to the next lender because the potential supplier failed to update the request), and, for article requests, whether or not the supplier has electronic document delivery capabilities (Ariel). A Microsoft Word macro queries the database and creates a new custom holdings list with one mouse click. Then the custom holdings are pasted into the OCLC ILL subsystem.

24. OCLC is working to implement this new directory in compliance with international standards. Phase one is scheduled for release early in 2003 according to Mark Tullos in "Policies Directory Update," [June 2002], <http://www.oclc.org/events/presentations/ala/policies.ppt> (12 January 2003). For more information on the standard, see Interlibrary Loan Application Standards Maintenance Agency, "Directory Services for Interlibrary Loan," 6 August 2002, <http://www.nlc-bnc.ca/iso/ill/ipd.htm> (12 January 2003).

25. OpenILL's home page is at <http://cybrary.uwinnipeg.ca/projects/openill/>. This page includes an impressive list of planned features. Mark Leggott states in "RE:

Information about OpenILL needed!" [3 January 2003], personal email (11 January 2003) that OpenILL partner libraries will be able to test an alpha product in January 2003, but that the software will not be available for "general consumption" until about two months later.

26. Raymond's first principle of bazaar-style open source development is that "Every good work of software starts by scratching a developer's personal itch," *Cathedral*, 23.

27. Chudnov, 43.

28. For more information on OCLC's open source initiatives, visit OCLC Research's "Software" page at <http://www.oclc.org/research/software/>.

29. "Infotrieve Acquires Ariel® Document Delivery Software," 22 January 2003, <http://www.infotrieve.com/ariel/acqinfo.html#Press>, (4 June 2003).

From Web Server to Portal: One Library's Experience with Open Source Software

Robert H. McDonald

Catherine M. Jannik

SUMMARY. Research libraries increasingly seek user-centered customizable library portals. Portal software allows seamless access and delivery of library electronic resources through either proprietary or open source portal solutions. This article examines the implementation of the MyLibrary open source portal software application at the Auburn University Libraries. It addresses the history of the open source movement and its place in library culture, particularly within research libraries. The Auburn Univer-

Robert H. McDonald is Assistant Director of Libraries for Technology, Media Services and Digital Libraries, Florida State University (E-mail: rmcdonal@mailer.fsu. edu; http://www.rmcdonald.info).

Catherine M. Jannik is Digital Initiatives Manager, Library and Information Center, Georgia Institute of Technology (E-mail: catherine.jannik@library.gatech.edu; http://www.jannik.us).

The authors would like to thank Kendall Price from the Auburn University Office of Information Technology and Beth Nicol from the Auburn University Library Technology Group for their time and expertise with Perl modules.

[Haworth co-indexing entry note]: "From Web Server to Portal: One Library's Experience with Open Source Software." McDonald, Robert H., and Catherine M. Jannik. Co-published simultaneously in *Journal of Library Administration* (The Haworth Information Press, an imprint of The Haworth Press, Inc.) Vol. 40, No. 1/2, 2004, pp. 71-87; and: *The Changing Landscape for Electronic Resources: Content, Access, Delivery, and Legal Issues* (ed: Yem S. Fong, and Suzanne M. Ward) The Haworth Information Press, an imprint of The Haworth Press, Inc., 2004, pp. 71-87. Single or multiple copies of this article are available for a fee from The Haworth Document Delivery Service [1-800-HAWORTH, 9:00 a.m. - 5:00 p.m. (EST). E-mail address: docdelivery@haworthpress.com].

sity Libraries' experience provides a case study for portal evaluation, selection, and implementation. The article also discusses the future implications of such systems. *[Article copies available for a fee from The Haworth Document Delivery Service: 1-800-HAWORTH. E-mail address: <docdelivery@haworthpress. com> Website: <http://www.HaworthPress.com> © 2004 by The Haworth Press, Inc. All rights reserved.]*

KEYWORDS. Open source software, MyLibrary, portals, electronic resources

INTRODUCTION

The University Libraries at Auburn University first installed the MyLibrary open source software portal in January 2001. Since then the Libraries have investigated and experimented with different avenues for user-customized portals as well as with the dissemination of electronic resources. One of the most important benefits of working with this software is the opportunity for exploring open source software and for offering new services to users.

Until the Auburn University Libraries implemented the MyLibrary software, the use of open source software within the libraries was generally limited to authentication scripts and network middleware. These types of projects were not seen as open source enterprise applications but as the middle layer of the Web services that were offered to our users. At the same time, the libraries had been running an Apache Web Server (open source project) to distribute electronic resources via the World Wide Web. In fact, the need for more seamless integration of electronic resources led directly to the investigation of portals.

This article offers an overview of open source software practices along with a corollary history of how open source initiatives have evolved in libraries, particularly in North American research libraries. The article also highlights the implementation of the MyLibrary software at the Auburn University Libraries and considers future directions and possibilities for open source and portal applications.

AN OPEN SOURCE OVERVIEW

Open source software (OSS) can be defined as that given freely, with accessible source code. In practice, the original developers release this software to a large user base that includes, possibly exclusively, other programmers who then become co-developers. Through their use of the software, bugs are ferreted out and solved, often by those who discover them but more often by other interested co-developer users. A very robust user base led by strong original developers leads to a dynamic but stable product. However, to understand OSS completely, one must know its history and the philosophy behind the OSS movement.

The definition of open source began as "The Debian Free Software Guidelines" by Bruce Perens. The definition evolved and references to Debian were removed, especially after comments by developers in a 1997 email conference. The refined explanation appears on the Open Source Software page as:

> Open source doesn't just mean access to the source code. The distribution terms of open-source software must comply with the following criteria:
>
> - The license shall not restrict any party from selling or giving away the software as a component of an aggregate software distribution containing programs from several different sources. The license shall not require a royalty or other fee for such sale.
> - The program must include source code, and must allow distribution in source code as well as compiled form. Where some form of a product is not distributed with source code, there must be a well-publicized means of obtaining the source code for no more than a reasonable reproduction cost-preferably, downloading via the Internet without charge. The source code must be the preferred form in which a programmer would modify the program. Deliberately obfuscated source code is not allowed. Intermediate forms such as the output of a preprocessor or translator are not allowed.
> - The license must allow modifications and derived works and must allow them to be distributed under the same terms as the license of the original software.
> - The license may restrict source code from being distributed in modified form *only* if the license allows the distribution of "patch files" with the source code for the purpose of modifying the program at build time. The license must explicitly permit distribution of software built from modified source code. The license may require derived works to carry a different name or version number from the original software.
> - The license must not discriminate against any person or group of persons.

- The license must not restrict anyone from making use of the program in a specific field of endeavor. For example, it may not restrict the program from being used in a business, or from being used for genetic research.
- The rights attached to the program must apply to all to whom the program is redistributed without the need for execution of an additional license by those parties.
- The license must not be specific to a product. The rights attached to the program must not depend on the program's being part of a particular software distribution. If the program is extracted from that distribution and used or distributed within the terms of the program's license, all parties to whom the program is redistributed should have the same rights as those that are granted in conjunction with the original software distribution.
- The license must not place restrictions on other software that is distributed along with the licensed software. For example, the license must not insist that all other programs distributed on the same medium must be open-source software.[1]

Richard Stallman founded the Free Software Foundation (FSF) in 1985. The foundation raises and provides funds for the GNU Project.[2] The title of his foundation is somewhat misleading because it does charge an initial distribution fee for GNU; future distributors are allowed to charge for cost recovery or profit. In the FSF model, "free" refers more to the freedom to modify and repackage software without restricting the freedom of the user. Though Stallman distinguishes free from open source software, he is still recognized as a major contributor to the movement.[3]

Stallman wrote the initial announcement for the GNU Project in 1983 and released it in January 1984. The announcement began:

> Starting this Thanksgiving I am going to write a complete UNIX-compatible software system called GNU (for Gnu's Not UNIX), and give it away free to everyone who can use it. Contributions of time, money, programs and equipment are greatly needed.[4]

It went on to explain some of the improvements over UNIX, that GNU would run UNIX programs, and the utilities that would be included. GNU was a complete clone of UNIX, the operating system based on work done at Bell Labs[5] by Ken Thompson and Dennis Ritchie in the late 1960s.[6]

Stallman's experiences with proprietary software motivated him to begin the project. While working at the Artificial Intelligence Laboratory at the Massachusetts Institute of Technology (MIT) during the 1970s and early 1980s, Stallman wanted to improve a printer driver and was unable to do so because the source code was closed. A nondisclosure agreement kept a colleague at another institution from sharing the source code for the driver. In addition the Artificial Intelligence Lab changed to a proprietary operating system which further frustrated Stallman's tinkering abilities. He resigned his position at MIT to begin work on GNU. The first release in early 1985 was available free of charge through an anonymous FTP site and by tape for $150. Thus to Stallman "free" does not indicate without cost but rather freedom to use GNU in whatever way the user deems appropriate.[7]

In 1991 Linus Torvalds, a Finnish hacker, announced his own free operating system for 386(486) AT clones that he called "just a hobby, won't be big and professional like GNU," based on a small UNIX-like operating system for PC clones called MINIX. Torvalds missed the mark with his announcement. The operating system he developed became Linux, considered as possibly the "only long-term challenge to the all-encompassing power of Microsoft."[8]

In "The Cathedral and the Bazaar," Eric Steven Raymond examines the theory of the open source methodology by detailing Torvalds' methods and success with developing Linux. Raymond compares the open source community and theory of development to "a great babbling bazaar of differing agendas and approaches."[9] In the traditional software development model Raymond notes that a very small number of programmers take an idea, develop the software, work out bugs, beta test, work out further bugs, and then release the product. After release, traditionally developed software then also goes through revisions that usually are not timely and that depend on non-programmer users' reports of bugs. This "cathedral-style" of development has a disadvantage at the general release stage when the non-programmer users try to describe the bugs they have encountered. Programmers experience programs in a different space than do users, and thus developers are often hard pressed to recreate a particular bug from an incident report from these uninitiated users.

The Torvalds "bazaar-style" of software development enables the developers to release often and early because its users are programmers and co-developers of software that they are also using. Users who are programmers are better able than non-programmer users to report the bugs they encounter, and they often help to develop the software by proposing solutions to these problems. Torvalds has said that in this model, "there is less of a 'buffer' between the user and the developer. The user can often *be* the developer . . ."[10] The developers of bazaar-style software are project managers in many senses and they incorporate other programmers' ideas and fixes into their original code. This approach embodies the adage that "two heads are better than one"; a developer too close to his own code can benefit from other eyes reviewing and using his product. Releases are more frequent and earlier than in the cathedral-style since fixes are constantly being incorporated and the user-developer does not expect the same type of finished product as from a commercial closed-source software company. In fact, Raymond explains that as necessary preconditions for developing software in the bazaar-style, one must have a "plausible promise."[11] Software destined for this type of development "can be crude, buggy, incomplete, and poorly documented. What it must not fail to do is (a) run, and (b) convince potential co-developers that it can be evolved into something really neat in the foreseeable future."[12]

OPEN SOURCE SOFTWARE IN LIBRARIES

Eric Lease Morgan, developer of the open source library portal software MyLibrary, explains that in relation to open source software, "the term 'free' should be more equated with the Latin word liberat (meaning to liberate), and not necessarily gratis (meaning without return made or expected)." He then equates the basic principles of open source software to American librarianship.[13]

Morgan addresses librarians' issues with utilizing open source by examining responses to a question posed on the oss4lib.org mailing list. Daniel Chudnov's domain, oss4lib.org, lists software designed for libraries such as Z39.50 clients and servers, library management systems, and document delivery applications and supports an accompanying electronic mailing list. Morgan specifically addresses national leadership, mainstreaming, workshops and training, usability and packaging, economic viability, redefinition of the integrated library system, and open source data. He sees the ability of librarians "to take control of library services and collections relying on computer software" with open source solutions as one of the most important possibilities.[14] Chudnov sees the limited resources of libraries, as well as the responsiveness of the community to calls for support, as good reasons for libraries to incorporate open source solutions. He also believes that the social nature of the library community makes the open source methodology a good fit.[15]

In addition, although open source requires more technical programming knowledge on the part of the systems administrators, less frequent patches and the relative stability and security of the software are valuable compensation. The distributed nature of the support throughout the community also virtually ensures that someone offering help is using the software for similar purposes. Although libraries have been slow to incorporate library specific open source solutions, open source database applications and server software have been widely incorporated throughout the library community.[16]

Chudnov explains that one of the reasons for libraries' problems with proprietary library systems is that the library community provides only a relatively small population to which the companies can sell their product. Librarians also tend not to upgrade as frequently as possible due to the high costs of migration, training, and support. With open source software, costs recouped from not having to purchase the software can be spent on such upgrades.[17]

FOUNDATIONS OF OPEN SOURCE SOFTWARE IN RESEARCH LIBRARIES

As Morgan has pointed out, there are many more ways that libraries can get involved in the OSS movement.[18] However, research libraries have historically been at the forefront of this movement because of their early adoption of management information systems. Since many research libraries are located at educational institutions that enabled early practitioners such as Stallman and Torvalds to create the core of the OSS movement, they have also contributed to distributed software development through the user group communities that often spring up around enterprise computing systems.[19]

These user groups closely mirrored groups that were forming around UNIX, GNU, and Linux. Most often the veteran users of the proprietary products would demonstrate solutions that they had created to work in conjunction with the proprietary product or propose a change to the source code of the proprietary product to offer more functionality for the user. These groups were often most beneficial to the creator and seller of the proprietary management system. However, many improvements to these systems did not have to be made in the source code; they were middleware pieces of software that often used open-source applications for implementation.[20] Many of these user groups hold annual meetings sponsored by the creator of the proprietary software.[21]

AUBURN UNIVERSITY LIBRARIES
AND OPEN SOURCE SOFTWARE

The Auburn University Libraries first became involved in the OSS movement soon after installing their first UNIX-based server for running the NOTIS library management system. This system, which was first created at Northwestern University, has many parallels with the type of work that Stallman describes at the MIT Artificial Intelligence lab.[22] The libraries using NOTIS were encouraged to develop solutions that could be shared and used by all libraries that had implemented the NOTIS system.[23] While running the UNIX operating system for NOTIS, those engaged in library systems began taking advantage of the developing standards that enabled UNIX systems to become part of the framework that eventually evolved into the modern day Internet.

As NOTIS grew and was replaced by more modern integrated library systems, such as Endeavor Information Systems' Voyager product, the changes in hardware and software further enhanced the way in which research libraries could become involved in OSS projects. A natural extension of the hardware/software needed to run an Oracle e-commerce application such as Voyager would simultaneously offer the ability to run the Apache Web Server. Once the Apache Web Server is up and running, the Internet becomes the pearl of the libraries' open source oyster and is the foundation for running most of the freely available Web based open source applications. The Apache OSS project directly involves more people every day over the Internet than nearly any other Web application, either open source or proprietary.

Once libraries began running Web servers, they began to see how electronic resources could be used outside of and in conjunction with the integrated library management system. This understanding led to other natural extensions, such as writing Perl and CGI scripts for electronic resource authentication methods. Institutions often shared these scripts as they improved and modified them. In effect, these scripts often serve as middleware between OSS Web applications and proprietary software, enabling libraries to control access to their electronic resources. Other OSS projects written specifically for libraries include portals, library management systems, Z39.50 servers, OAI metadata harvesters, and brokers, just to name a few.[24]

It seems only natural that out of this environment of sharing, the Auburn University Libraries embraced the concept of open source applications and techniques and was the foundation for becoming involved with the MyLibrary OSS project. At Auburn, current systems integral to MyLibrary include: Linux OS, Apache Web Server, MySQL, Perl, PHP, and MyLibrary.

PORTAL EVALUATION

When the Auburn University Libraries began looking at solutions to create a user-customized electronic resource portal, staff considered many types of products before deciding on an open source implementation. The Libraries viewed the implementation of a user-customized portal as an experimental project and did not want to overlook any useful products. At the same time, the Auburn University Libraries did not want to invest heavily in the infrastructure required to run the portal. Staff evaluated several products in late 2000, including out-of-the-box library system solutions, customizable products, and open source projects.[25] Only one product, MyLibrary, fit the open-source model.[26] These are the products that staff evaluated, by category:

Out-of-the-Box

Autonomy Inc.–Portal in a Box
<http://www.autonomy.com/Content/Products/Interfaces/PIB/>
Fretwell Downing Inc.–ZPORTAL
<http://www.fdusa.com/products/zportal.html>

Customizable Products

OCLC Inc.–SiteSearch
<http://www.sitesearch.oclc.org/>[27]

Open Source Solutions

MyLibrary–
<http://dewey.library.nd.edu/mylibrary/>[28]

From the evaluations of these products, the library discovered that each would take similar amounts of time for implementation and maintenance. Each package required the installation of at least one new piece of hardware. Also, each portal package required both a steep learning curve for the administration of the portal software as well as a considerable amount of time devoted to customizing the package to meet the needs of Auburn library constituents. These factors proved to be true for all three categories of software.[29] However, what ultimately led to the open source solution was that it was designed with libraries in mind. This solution required less initial customization than the other packages and, because it ran on an open source operating system, the software could be tested on existing equipment before investing in the hardware that would run the production version of the portal. There was also a significant price difference in the hardware and operating system platforms required for running the production version of the open source solution and the hardware and licensing fees of other products. The Linux operating system requires no licensing fee and is available via a variety of anonymous FTP sites while other versions of UNIX often require proprietary hardware as well as extensive licensing fees.[30]

MyLibrary AT AUBURN UNIVERSITY LIBRARIES

The implementation of an open source portal at Auburn University Libraries is presented as a case study. Implementation of open source software requires varying degrees of knowledge, time, and commitment depending on the platform on which the program will be run, the needs of the organization, and other factors that arise in the implementation of enterprise-wide software systems. Under the leadership of Dean Stella Bentley, Auburn University Libraries implemented Eric Lease Morgan's MyLibrary Portal first in a trial phase and later moved to a production version. The impetus for this implementation was four-fold. First, the user community expressed a need for tighter integration of electronic resources. Secondly, the Auburn University campus had been discussing implementation of an enterprise-wide portal for some time and Robert H. McDonald, the Information Technology Librarian, had been interested in the library taking a leading role in the content of this portal. At the same time, following a meeting with other Association of Research Libraries (ARL) directors, Stella Bentley determined that an information portal was a natural outcome for Auburn University Libraries. Finally, the libraries' focus groups and usability testing initiatives clearly indicated that users had a critical need for some type of unification of electronic resources.

Planning

After preliminary investigation of the technical aspects of this project, the libraries began the planning process for an enterprise-wide implementation. This process required input from many areas, especially from public services and reference departments. The information technology librarian took the lead in presenting the benefits of the system to various library departments.

Presentations were made to the reference department, library department heads, and the collection development team, as well as to focus groups comprised of both faculty and students at Auburn University. These presentations emphasized the need for electronic resource integration and the benefits that an information portal could offer. During these information sessions the presenter summarized the evaluations of the products that had been reviewed and emphasized the reasons for choosing MyLibrary. At the same time, policy issues for the portal began to emerge. All three library groups felt that the portal should be as open as possible so that any user group could subscribe to the service. The faculty and student focus groups felt that the login should be as easy as possible. These issues formed the basis for establishing another group to look at policy issues for the portal. This policy group included the information technology librarian, the electronic resources librarian, and the head of collection development.

Implementation and Content Maintenance

With two implementation groups, one policy and one technical, and the library community on board with the concept of a user-customized portal, the library began experimenting with the MyLibrary software using a Dell Computer Corporation GX1 desktop computer equipped with an Intel Pentium II processor running the Red Hat Linux operating system. This system, with minimal amounts of RAM and storage space, was sufficient for serving as a test bed for most open source software packages that run on a variety of SQL databases.[31] At the same time, the library began to configure the hardware needed to run this portal in a production mode, using a Dell Poweredge 4400 server running Red Hat Linux. The library acquired the new hardware for $4,000.[32]

At this stage, the most challenging part of implementation was installing the Perl modules in the right order for them to work with both the MySQL back-end database and the Apache Web Server front-end. While this procedure is not complicated, first-timers should install each module separately rather than try to use the CPAN module that can install all these modules at once.[33] The expertise for installing the Perl modules came from within the library technology department. The library also received invaluable consultation from Auburn University's Office of Information Technology.[34]

The two other major challenges were authentication for electronic resources and content maintenance. The authentication method already in place used URL redirects and EZProxy, a rewriting proxy server.[35] Using this system anyone could create a customized portal page. For proprietary electronic resources, Auburn University affiliated students and personnel needed a login method to gain access remotely from any type of Internet connection. At the same time, anyone who accessed the portal from within the Auburn University Internet Protocol domain range would automatically connect to the resource with no need for the proxy service.

The content maintenance solution closely mirrored the electronic resources vetting process currently in operation in the libraries. Slight changes were needed so that collection development librarians could suggest additions of free non-paid electronic resources.[36] Content maintenance of portal resources was initially centralized so that there would be less confusion between collection development librarians and the technology group. Another reason for centralization was because the library technology group was also testing how to load the Auburn University electronic journal titles automatically from the library catalog system.

Portal Promotion

When publicizing MyLibrary@Auburn, the library used a "What's New" electronic mailing list and an accompanying web page, a scrolling marquee on the libraries' home page, bibliographic instruction classes, and the library's liaison program.[37] In addition, an entire day of the libraries' National Library Week activities was dedicated to MyLibrary and the logo was put on t-shirts for the libraries' annual 5K run. Continuing publicity is accomplished with a permanent link on the libraries' home page, instruction sessions, liaison activities, and prominent placement of the logo on libraries' event shirts and posters.

These events have been very successful in generating use of the MyLibrary portal and have also generated other ideas for use with the portal. Such novel uses include generating static HTML research link pages that are then published and distributed through the university's online learning management system, WebCT. These link pages enable instructors to identify easily the best electronic resources that the libraries have to offer and to create a web page that can then be uploaded to the learning management system that instructors use with their classes. For students, the link pages also mean that all of the electronic information resources that they need show up with one login to the course web page. Currently there are over 600 registered users for MyLibrary@Auburn University.

FUTURE DIRECTIONS

While the MyLibrary portal at Auburn University has not gained wide spread acceptance, it has developed a small devoted following.[38] The successful implementation of this open source portal has inspired the library to think of how such an information portal could be tied in with a future enterprise-wide university portal. Customizable methods of accessing information can be thought of as information channels. Imagine a day where all students in Chemistry or English can log into a university-wide portal that enables customizable and one-click access to the best information resources available from the library specific to their major field of study. If this access is possible in an environment that makes available registration information and due dates for projects and exams, the library can inject itself into specific and tangible learning outcomes for students.

Other recent changes in integrated library information systems have included customizable bookbags in library OPACs, personal image directories via image management systems, and personalized saved searches within library databases and multi-search platforms. These enhancements indicate that users want these types of options and that libraries are in a unique position to provide them. However, these types of personalized services and electronic resources need to be integrated for seamless access. Could this be a call for a personalization feature within a Web OPAC that includes a management module for electronic resources? Many library vendors hear this call and yet do not see how this type of system can work for the user. A development partnership between universities, their libraries, and a major library system vendor could spur this type of development. Collaboration could encourage universities to work with libraries in building their research information channel that would sit alongside and complement other university information channels on a university-wide portal. Learning management systems are quickly becoming major repositories of the university's intellectual output. These systems will suffer without better standards for long-term preservation and open access, and thoughtful planning for more enterprise-wide interoperability.[39]

Libraries are also discovering how a university authentication service built into the university-wide learning management system can enable seamless access to an OSS portal such as MyLibrary. These efforts are being considered along with more robust authentication systems such as Shibboleth.[40] Shared authentication systems can offer an infrastructure for faculty and students to access their own customized university and library information channels if the university decides to implement a university-wide portal.[41]

CONCLUSION

In the past, libraries have often viewed open source software projects as experimental and as not scalable for projects of a certain size. Having many times looked first to proprietary commercial software to provide solutions and support for library electronic services, libraries failed to see the communities of developers working on projects that would benefit their users. However, by looking at the traditional role that technology staff have played in research libraries and their ties to the open source community, it became clear for one library that for certain projects that can scale to appropriate capacity, open source software initiatives can provide all of the benefits of commercial software without all of the initial startup costs that some commercial products bring with them. And while open source software is not free from requiring human expertise and skill sets, it can provide a test bed enabling experimentation and learning for future library services and applications.

NOTES

1. OpenSource.org., The Open Source Definition, Version 1.9 8, 2002, <http://www.opensource.org/docs/definition.php> [cited 4 November 2002].

2. Free Software Foundation <http://www.fsf.org/fsf/fsf.html> and the GNU Project <http://www.gnu.org/gnu/thegnuproject.html>.

3. "GNU-a whatis definition," 2002, <http://whatis.techtarget.com/definition/0,,sid9_gci212202,00.html>, [cited 12 December 2002].

4. Richard Stallman, "Initial Announcement-GNU Project," Free Software Foundation (FSF), 1999, <http://www.gnu.org/gnu/initial-announcement.html>, [cited 12 December 2002].

5. Bell Labs is now the research and development arm of Lucent Technologies Inc. It was formerly part of AT&T Corp. before the breakup of the Bell System in 1984.

6. For a history of UNIX Eric S. Raymond, "A Brief History of Hackerdom," 2000, <http://www.tuxedo.org/~esr/writings/hacker-history/>, [cited 12 December 2002].

7. David W. Bretthauer, "Open Source Software: A History," *Information Technology and Libraries* 21 (1), (Mar. 2002): 3-10. [cited 17 October 2002]. Available from FirstSearch, WilsonSelectPlus Full Text, Dublin, OH.

8. Richard Poynder, "The Open Source Movement: Does this software provide a viable, user-friendly alternative to proprietary solutions?" *Information Today* 18 (9), (Oct. 2001): 67-69. [cited 12 December 2002]. Available online at <http://www.infotoday.com/it/oct01/poynder.htm>.

9. Eric Steven Raymond, "The Cathedral and the Bazaar." [cited 12 December 2002]. Available online at <http://www.tuxedo.org/~esr/writings/cathedral-bazaar/>.

10. Rishab Aiyer Ghosh, "FM Interview with Linus Torvalds: What Motivates Free Software Developers?" *First Monday* 3 (3), (March 1998). [cited 17 October 2002]. Available online at <http://www.firstmonday.dk/issues/issue3_3/torvalds/index.html>.

11. Raymond, "Cathedral."

12. Raymond, "Cathedral."

13. Eric Lease Morgan, "Possibilities for Open Source Software in Libraries," *Information Technology and Libraries* 21 (1), (Mar. 2002): 12-15. [cited 30 December 2002]. Available from FirstSearch WilsonSelectPlus Full Text, Dublin, OH.

14. Morgan, "Possibilities."

15. Bill Mickey, "Open Source and Libraries: An Interview with Dan Chudnov," *Online* 25 (1), (Jan./Feb. 2001): 23-8. [cited 17 October 2002]. Available from FirstSearch, WilsonSelectPlus Full Text, Dublin, OH.

16. John Creech, "Open Source Software @ the CWU Library," *PNLA Quarterly* 65 (4), (Summer 2001): 15-17. [cited 17 October 2002]. Available from FirstSearch, WilsonSelectPlus Full Text, Dublin, OH.

17. Dan Chudnov, "Open Source Software: The Future of Library Systems?" *Library Journal* 124 (13), (August 1999): 40-3. [cited 17 October 2002]. Available from FirstSearch, WilsonSelectPlus Full Text, Dublin, OH.

18. Morgan, "Possibilities."

19. The groups include the old NUG (NOTIS User Group), VUG (Voyager User Group), and now EndUser Group (Endeavor User Group) as well as the AUG (Aleph User Group) and SMUG (SFX and Metalib User Group).

20. Examples of this type of implementation are Michael Doran's new book list software that works in conjunction with the database tables in the Voyager Library Management System. Also such groups as SMUGNET put templates online that can be modified by users to save time in the creation of configurations for use with SFX.

21. These types of meetings are similar in scope to other open source based conferences such as LinuxWorld and ApacheCon.

22. David Bennahum, "Interview with Richard Stallman," *MEME* 2.04. [online newsletter]. [cited 17 December 2002]. Available online at <http://memex.org/meme2-04.html>.

23. NOTIS was eventually turned into a for-profit business by Northwestern and eventually sold to Ameritech. This turn away from open source techniques combined with changes in technology eventually led to its demise.

24. Open Archives Initiative. See <http://www.openarchives.org>.

25. As this evaluation was undertaken in 1999-2000 the products mentioned are dated and should be re-evaluated before being used for such a portal project.

26. Since this installation there have been several other portal products that have evolved within the open source community. These include the Internet Scout Project Portal Toolkit <http://scout.wisc.edu/research/SPT/> and uPortal <http://mis105.mis.udel.edu/ja-sig/uportal/>.

27. Since our investigation of SiteSearch this product has become available in an open source project for non-commercial uses. This was due in large part to the phenomenal success of SiteSearch and to the investment in infrastructure that many libraries made to this product.

28. MyLibrary was originally developed at North Carolina State University Libraries and has since moved along with Eric Lease Morgan to the Notre Dame University Libraries <http://dewey.library.nd.edu/mylibrary/>.

29. All of the software that we evaluated would have required significant amount of time for initial customization unless we had spent funding contracting with the vendor or outside consultants.

30. At the time of our evaluation only SiteSearch and MyLibrary would run on the Linux open source platform. The other products required proprietary hardware from Sun Microsystems Inc. and the necessary licensing fees to run the Sun version of UNIX called Solaris.

31. SQL stands for structured query language. This query language allows relational databases to share data. The MyLibrary portal uses the open source MySQL database software.

32. Note that this figure is just for hardware costs. The software costs are minimal however the systems administration time required for the set-up for both the test server and the production server was the most expensive part of this project.

33. CPAN is a Perl module that can download and install other Perl modules on your server. Using CPAN requires a typical server configuration and a familiarity with Perl modules.

34. Perl is an open source project developed by Larry Wall in 1987. It is an extensive open source project that has many different modules capable of performing many different tasks in a UNIX/Linux environment.

35. See appendix.

36. This is not the only option for running a subject-based portal. In fact, having each collection developer or subject specialist maintain his or her individual subject areas is probably a better model.

37. This electronic mailing list and its accompanying web page are used by the Auburn University Libraries to promote new services to its users.

38. Only 2.5% of our total student and faculty (23,600 total) use the service.

39. Clifford Lynch, "The Afterlives of Courses on the Network: Information Management Issues for Learning Management Systems." *ECAR Research Bulletin 2002* (3), (November 26, 2002). [cited 4 January 2003]. Available online at <http://www.cni.org/tfms/2002b.fall/abstracts/PB-Afterlives-Lynch.html>.

40. Shibboleth is a middleware project being developed by the Internet2 MACE committee. This authentication system will enable seamless access to many different information resources for members of university communities utilizing local university information resources, learning management systems, and library research databases.

41. As of this writing the uPortal open source university-wide portal project is increasingly being implemented by many major universities. See <http://mis105.mis.udel.edu/ja-sig/uportal/>.

APPENDIX. MyLibrary@Auburn Authentication/Access Diagram

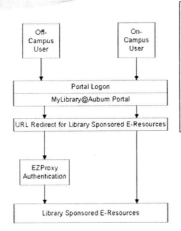

MyLibrary@Auburn
Authentication/Access Diagram

| Off-Campus User | On-Campus User |

Note that any user can register for a MyLibrary@Auburn account but only authorized users can connect to Library Paid E-Resources.

Free/Open Resources do not use URL Redirects so are direct links for all users.

Portal Logon

MyLibrary@Auburn Portal

URL Redirect for Library Sponsored E-Resources

EZProxy Authentication

Library Sponsored E-Resources

Recent Developments in Standards for Resource Sharing

Julie Blume Nye

SUMMARY. This article discusses important new developments related to the three core standards that underpin resource sharing and interlibrary loan. Topics include the Bath Profile and U.S. National Profile for Z39.50; the IPIG-OCLC ILL Policies Directory, the Request Submission Message used in conjunction with the ILL Protocol; and Z39.83, the new NISO Circulation Interchange Protocol (NCIP). *[Article copies available for a fee from The Haworth Document Delivery Service: 1-800-HAWORTH. E-mail address: <docdelivery@haworthpress.com> Website: <http://www.HaworthPress.com> © 2004 by The Haworth Press, Inc. All rights reserved.]*

KEYWORDS. Standards, Z39.50, Bath Profile, interlibrary loan protocol, NCIP, circulation

INTRODUCTION

This article discusses important new developments related to core standards underpinning resource sharing and interlibrary loan. Two of those core standards, Z39.50 and ISO 10160/10161, should be familiar

Julie Blume Nye is Senior Product Designer, Fretwell-Downing, Inc. (E-mail: julie.nye@fdgroup.com).

[Haworth co-indexing entry note]: "Recent Developments in Standards for Resource Sharing." Nye, Julie Blume. Co-published simultaneously in *Journal of Library Administration* (The Haworth Information Press, an imprint of The Haworth Press, Inc.) Vol. 40, No. 1/2, 2004, pp. 89-106; and: *The Changing Landscape for Electronic Resources: Content, Access, Delivery, and Legal Issues* (ed: Yem S. Fong, and Suzanne M. Ward) The Haworth Information Press, an imprint of The Haworth Press, Inc., 2004, pp. 89-106. Single or multiple copies of this article are available for a fee from The Haworth Document Delivery Service [1-800-HAWORTH, 9:00 a.m. - 5:00 p.m. (EST). E-mail address: docdelivery@haworthpress.com].

http://www.haworthpress.com/web/JLA
© 2004 by The Haworth Press, Inc. All rights reserved.
Digital Object Identifier: 10.1300/J111v40n01_07

to readers of this journal, at least by number. Although the standards themselves have not changed recently, there have been important agreements and developments *related* to the standards. And there is now a third core standard: Z39.83, the new NISO Circulation Interchange Protocol (NCIP).

Z39.50–SEARCH AND RETRIEVAL

Z39.50 is well known within the library community as the standard for searching online catalogs and other databases. Now in Version 3, Z39.50 defines a standard way for two computers to communicate and share information, whether that information is bibliographic data, full-text documents, images or multimedia. Technically, there are two identical standards, *ANSI/NISO Z39.50-1995 Information Retrieval: Application Service Definition & Protocol Specification* in the United States and *ISO 23950:1998 Information and Documentation–Information retrieval (Z39.50)–Application service definition and protocol specification* internationally. The standard is based on client-server architecture, but uses the terms "origin" and "target" when referring to client and server, respectively.

NISO approved a maintenance revision of the Z39.50 standard in 2002, but changes were relatively minor and should not affect current implementations. Z39.50 as a standard is relatively mature, and Version 3 has been widely implemented. Recent developments relating to Z39.50 are in two areas: ZING and implementation profiles.

ZING–Z39.50 INTERNATIONAL:
NEXT GENERATION

ZING includes several related efforts by implementers worldwide "to make Z39.50 more attractive to information providers outside the mainstream library automation community." Each ZING project is intended to simplify one or more aspects of Z39.50 implementation while retaining the power and flexibility of the original protocol. None of the ZING initiatives are commercial products yet.

Current ZING initiatives are SRW (including SRU), CQL, ZOOM, ez3950, and ZeeRex. Some (for example, SRW/SRU) seek to evolve Z39.50 to a more mainstream protocol using web services, while for others (e.g., ZOOM) the purpose is to preserve the existing protocol but hide its complexity.[1] More information about each initiative is available at the ZING area of the Z39.50 Maintenance Agency web site.[2]

Z39.50 IMPLEMENTATION PROFILES

Of more immediate interest is the development of profiles for implementing Z39.50. Although Z39.50 has been available in commercial implementations since the early 1990s, even today a common complaint among librarians is that search results obtained using Z39.50 are inconsistent or unreliable. Upon closer examination, it becomes apparent that these problems are not caused by defects in the standards themselves, but are due to differences in the way libraries index their bibliographic records, and to differences in the way automation vendors have configured their Z39.50 products. Implementation profiles attempt to minimize these differences and improve the accuracy and precision of results when searching multiple targets.

Within any standard there are implementation options, and the meaning of some specifications may be open to interpretation. Implementation profiles identify a subset of specifications (e.g., selected services and required values for specific parameters) that are to be used in specific applications. Profiles therefore provide the mechanism for vendors and users with an interest in common functionality to specify a standard way to interpret and implement options within a standard.

The earliest Z39.50 profiles were developed by implementers outside the mainstream library community: examples include the GILS profile for government information locator services and the CIMI profile for exchange of museum and cultural heritage information. Several European library groups have developed national and multinational profiles. The first North American profile, the Z Texas Profile, appeared in early 1999.

The Bath and U.S. National Profiles are the most recent and, for North American readers, the most significant developments in Z39.50 profiling. Both profiles specify what kind of searches must be available to users, how searches must be constructed by the client for transmission to the target, and what record syntax must be used to return the results.[3]

Both profiles describe multiple levels of conformance (compliance), and several functional areas. Vendors may choose to implement some or all functional areas, and may implement different functional areas at different levels of conformance. Librarians need to become familiar with both profiles in order to ask the right questions in Requests for Proposals (RFPs) and to understand system vendors' claims of profile compliance.

NISO's recently published *RFP Writer's Guide to Standards for Library Systems* includes both the U.S. National and Bath profiles in its excellent chapter on Z39.50 (Chapter VIII, Information Retrieval).[4]

Bath Profile

Named for the English city where its development began in August 1999, the Bath Profile is subtitled *An International Z39.50 Specification for Library Applications and Resource Discovery.*[5] According to the FAQ:

> *The Bath Profile* identifies those features of the Z39.50 standard required to support effective use of Z39.50 software for a range of library functions, such as basic searching and retrieval of bibliographic records for cataloguing, interlibrary loan, reference, and acquisitions. The profile defines both a core set of basic author, title and subject search and retrieval specifications across a variety of library databases, and a set of more complex searches. The functionality and specifications identified in the profile are intended to be incorporated into more detailed national, regional, provincial/state, and local agreements.[6]

The Bath Profile is an Internationally Registered Profile (IRP) but not a NISO or ISO standard. There is no formal approval process for revisions. Release 2.0 was published in March 2003 and covers four functional areas:

- Functional Area A: Bibliographic Search and Retrieval, with Primary Focus on Library Catalogues
- Functional Area B: Bibliographic Holdings Search and Retrieval
- Functional Area C: Cross-Domain Search and Retrieval
- Functional Area D: Authority Record Search and Retrieval in Online Library Catalogues

Systems may support one or more functional areas. The Bath Profile also describes three levels of conformance:

- Level 0–encompasses many existing products but may require reconfiguration
- Level 1–extends functionality and interoperability; RFPs for new systems should specify at least this level
- Level 2–more demanding requirements; should guide system enhancements and development of new functionality

Conformance levels are defined separately for each functional area, and there is no requirement that conformant systems must conform at the same level in each functional area supported. Conformance requirements are inherited, that is, Level 1 conformance requires support for all Level 0 requirements in addition to the requirements specified for Level 1.

Search Example

To illustrate how Bath Profile conformance will improve the accuracy of search results, consider the following example:

```
@attr 1=1003 harris
```

This is a valid Z39.50 author search for "harris," as formatted for the Yaz Z39.50 client. "@attr 1" indicates the type of search, and the value 1003 means "author."

The Z39.50 standard specifies six different attributes that may be included in the query:

- attribute 1 (use), e.g., author, subject heading, ISBN[7]
- attribute 2 (relation), e.g., equal, greater than
- attribute 3 (position), e.g., any position in field, first in subfield
- attribute 4 (structure), e.g., word, phrase, date
- attribute 5 (truncation), e.g., do not truncate, right truncation
- attribute 6 (completeness), e.g., incomplete subfield, complete field

The Z39.50 standard does not require that values for all six attributes be included in a search query, so the target must make assumptions about any attributes that are not specified. Not surprisingly, different targets make different assumptions. In the example above, the value of attribute 5 (truncation) was not specified. Some targets will assume that the search term is *not* to be truncated; other targets will assume the term *is* to be truncated. Search results from the latter will include authors named Harrison. Either assumption is valid and represents standard-compliant behavior.

The Bath Profile and related profiles eliminate this ambiguity by requiring that *every query include a value for every attribute.*

```
@attr 1=1003 @attr 2=2 @attr 3=3  @attr 4=2 @attr 5=100

              @attr 6=1 harris
```

This is a much more precise search than the earlier example:

- attribute 1 (use) = 1003 (author)
- attribute 2 (relation) = 2 (equal)
- attribute 3 (position) = 3 (any position in field)
- attribute 4 (structure) = 2 (word)
- attribute 5 (truncation) = 100 (do not truncate)
- attribute 6 (completeness) = 1 (incomplete subfield)

This is Bath Profile query *5.A.0.1. Author Search–Keyword*, a requirement for Level 0 conformance in Functional Area A. The U.S. National Profile also requires this search (designated BP0.1) for Level 0 conformance.

As indicated by the qualifiers "Bibliographic Search and Retrieval" in their names, Functional Areas A and B were developed for searching library catalogs. Table 1 lists the searches required in Functional Area A. In addition to twenty-five searches, systems must also support the Z39.50 Scan service for browsing by author, title and subject. Functional Area B requires no additional searches but defines three "element set names" for retrieval of holdings information at differing levels of detail.

Functional Area C is intended for cross-domain searching of networked resources, including library catalogs, government information, museum systems, and archives. It defines thirteen searches, many of which mirror searches in Functional Area A, and requires targets to return results using the Dublin Core metadata element set.

Functional Area D defines an array of searches and scans for specific types of names, titles and subject headings in authority records. A total of 54 searches and 6 scans are specified.

U.S. National Profile

The U.S. National Profile also describes its requirements in terms of separate functional areas, each with three levels of conformance. Very similar to the Bath Profile, at least in the functional areas they have in common (A and B), the U.S. National Profile requires a larger number

TABLE 1. Bath Profile Searches: Functional Area A, Bibliographic Search and Retrieval with Primary Focus on Library Catalogues

Level 0

5.A.0.1.	Author Search–Keyword
5.A.0.2.	Title Search–Keyword
5.A.0.3.	Subject Search–Keyword
5.A.0.4.	Any Search–Keyword[8]

Level 1

5.A.1.1.	Author Search–Keyword with Right Truncation
5.A.1.2.	Author Search–Exact Match
5.A.1.3.	Author Search–First Words in Field
5.A.1.4.	Author Search–First Characters in Field
5.A.1.5.	Title Search–Keyword with Right Truncation
5.A.1.6.	Title Search–Exact Match
5.A.1.7.	Title Search–First Words in Field
5.A.1.8.	Title Search–First Characters in Field
5.A.1.9.	Subject Search–Keyword with Right Truncation
5.A.1.10.	Subject Search–Exact Match
5.A.1.11.	Subject Search–First Words in Field
5.A.1.12.	Subject Search–First Characters in Field
5.A.1.13.	Any Search–Keyword with Right Truncation
5.A.1.14.	Standard Identifier Search
5.A.1.15.	Date of Publication Search
5.A.1.SCAN.1.	Author–Exact Match
5.A.1.SCAN.2.	Title–Exact Match
5.A.1.SCAN.3.	Subject–Exact Match

Level 2

5.A.2.1.	Key Title Search–Keyword
5.A.2.2.	Key Title Search–Keyword with Right Truncation
5.A.2.3.	Key Title Search–Exact Match
5.A.2.4.	Key Title Search–First Words in Field
5.A.2.5.	Key Title Search–First Characters in Field
5.A.2.6.	Format/Type of Material Search–Keyword
5.A.2.7.	Format/Type of Material Search–Phrase
5.A.2.8.	Language Search–Keyword
5.A.2.9.	Date of Publication Range Search
5.A.2.10.	Possessing Institution Search

of searches, and for this reason is considered a "compatible superset" of the Bath Profile.

It is important to note that the U.S. National profile is to some extent a work in progress. Approved by NISO ballot in March 2003, the profile is officially designated ANSI/NISO *Z39.89–The U.S. National Z39.50 Profile for Library Applications.*[9] The first release covers Functional Area A.

Seventy-five searches are specified for Functional Area A, twenty-six of which correspond exactly to searches in the Bath Profile, Functional Area A. Table 2 summarizes the searches required at each conformance level.

XML Holdings Schema and Functional Area B

A holdings schema for use with Z39.50 was first adopted by the Z39.50 Implementors Group (ZIG) in 1999 and is required under Functional Area B of the Bath Profile, but consistent inclusion of holdings information in search results has continued to be problematic. The U.S. profile committee's work on Functional Area B includes further development of an XML Holdings Schema originally developed in Denmark for the ONE-2 interoperability project. The XML Holdings Schema promises a more tightly standardized way to return detailed holdings information from Z39.50 searches.

A schema is defined simply as an abstract record structure, in other words, a hypothetical representation of the structure of a record. Despite the existence of the MARC Format for Holdings, the representation of holdings information in library catalogs still varies widely from system to system, and even between different libraries' implementation of the same system. The XML holdings schema defines a format for returning holdings in Z39.50 search results, regardless of how holdings data are actually represented in each of the local systems searched.

In the case of a broadcast search to multiple targets, each target would map its local holdings data onto the XML holdings schema when sending back its search results. Because the data are returned in a mutually understood and highly structured format, the origin should be able to display holdings to the user in a consistent way for all targets searched. Results structured according to the XML holdings schema would also be available for further processing by the origin (client), for example, combining results from all targets searched to create a summarized holdings display.

Functional Area B requirements in the U.S. National Profile will probably not differ greatly from those in the Bath Profile. No additional

TABLE 2. U.S. National Profile Searches: Functional Area A, Bibliographic Search and Retrieval

Level 0

BP0.1	Author Search–Keyword
BP0.2	Title Search–Keyword
BP0.3	Subject Search–Keyword
BP0.4	Any Search–Keyword

Level 1

BP1.1-1.4	Author Search–4 types
BP1.5-1.8	Title Searches–4 types
BP1.9-1.12	Subject Searches–4 types
BP1.13	Any Search–Keyword with Right Truncation
BP1.14	Standard Identifier Search
US1.1	ISBN Search
US1.2	ISSN Search
US1.3	Remote System Record Number Search
BP1.15	Date of Publication Search
US1.4	Language Search
US1.5	Format of Material Search–Keyword
BP1.SCAN.1	Author–Exact Match
BP1.SCAN.2	Title–Exact Match
BP1.SCAN.3	Subject–Exact Match

Level 2

BP2.1-2.5	Key Title Search–5 types
US2.1-2.5	Uniform Title Searches–5 types
US2.6-2.10	Series Title Searches–5 types
US2.11	Title Search–Unanchored Phrase
US2.12	Subject Search–Unanchored Phrase
US2.13	Name Search–Unanchored Phrase
US2.14	Any Search–Unanchored Phrase
US2.15	Type of Material Search–Keyword
BP2.6	Date of Publication Range Search
US2.16	LCCN Search
US2.17	OCLC Number Search
US2.18	Music Publisher Number Search
US2.19	International Standard Music Number (ISMN) Search
US2.20	Technical Report Number Search

TABLE 2 (continued)

US2.21-2.22	Government Documents Searches–2 types
US2.23-2.24	Notes Searches–2 types
US2.25	Publisher Name Search–Keyword
BP2.7	Possessing Institution Search
US2.26-2.29	Personal Author Search–4 types
US2.30-2.33	Corporate Author Searches–4 types
US2.34-2.37	Conference Author Search–4 types
US2.38-2.41	Controlled Vocabulary Search–4 types

searches are likely to be required, but the most recent draft does define three element set names for presentation of search results, each of which is a subset of the XML Holdings Schema:

US ESN-1   Minimum (title-level) holdings
US ESN-2   Summary level holdings
US ESN-3   Extended piece-level holdings

The U.S. ESNs differ somewhat from their counterparts in the Bath Profile. Functional Area B of the U.S. National Profile may be issued separately during 2003 as a Draft Standard for Trial Use (DSFTU).[10]

ISO 10160/10161–ILL PROTOCOL

Like the Z39.50 standard, the ILL Protocol itself is a mature standard. Collectively known simply as "the ILL Protocol," the standard is described in two separate documents, ISO *10160:1997 Information and Documentation–Open Systems Interconnection–Interlibrary Loan Application Service Definition* and *ISO 10161-2:1997 Information and Documentation–Open Systems Interconnection–Interlibrary Loan Application Protocol Specification–Part 1: Protocol Specification.*

A revised version is under discussion within the ILL Protocol Implementers' Group (IPIG) but publication, balloting, and implementation are still several years away. Two other IPIG initiatives are of more immediate interest: the development of an international Interlibrary Loan Policies Directory, and the new IPIG Patron Request Submission Message. Information about the ILL protocol and related initiatives is available at the ILL Protocol Maintenance Agency web site.[11]

DIRECTORY SERVICES FOR INTERLIBRARY LOAN

Over the past two years, IPIG members developed a schema for representing interlibrary loan policy and contact information in a structured format that could be interpreted by ILL management software and could be exchanged between systems. Discussions are currently underway with OCLC to host a cooperative ILL Policies Directory for the IPIG. Several national policy directories are already online or under development, but an IPIG-OCLC directory would be a significant milestone for several reasons:

- international in scope/will complement national policy directories where such exist
- not limited to libraries that use a particular ILL system
- not limited by type of library or consortium membership
- accessible to ILL management software in addition to staff

OCLC had already planned to replace its Name and Address Directory (NAD), which included interlibrary loan policy information in a mostly free-text format. Adopting the "Directory Services for Interlibrary Loan" schema and hosting the cooperative directory would be logical next steps.

Several key technical details still await resolution, but it is expected that the cooperative directory will include two interfaces: a web interface for library staff who wish to search the directory manually and/or update their institution's policy information; and a machine interface for ILL management systems (like Fretwell-Downing's VDX) to search while processing requests, and for synchronizing local requester and supplier policy information with the cooperative directory.

Table 3 summarizes the data elements in the Directory Services for Interlibrary Loan schema. The IPIG web sute provides extensive documentation, including the latest information model and the XML schema for download.[12]

REQUEST SUBMISSION MESSAGE

The ILL Protocol defines a suite of messages to be exchanged between a requesting library and a supplier. Originally developed in the years before patron-initiated requesting was common, the protocol does not specify the data elements to be used when a patron submits a request to the library.

TABLE 3. Directory Services for Interlibrary Loan: Summary of Information Included in the Schema

ILL Unit

    Name, symbols, aliases, affiliations
    Contact information
    Types of requesters served, request methods accepted
    Services offered
- types and levels of service
- hours of availability
- charges
- payment and billing options
- material types
- delivery methods

    Loan policies

- collections available
- loan period
- renewal, overdue, replacement policies
- maximum submissions
- use restrictions
- return instructions

    Copy policies

- collections available
- medium types
- copy methods available
- copyright/rights management information
- maximum submissions
- max/min pages

    Policies for other services (e.g., locations, cost estimate)

Many libraries have implemented online request forms for patrons as a page on the library's web site, or as a function within the online catalog or search gateway. In the absence of a standard for patron-initiated requests, many libraries' online forms are simply automated versions of the library's paper ILL form. Others have based their online forms on the data elements in the ILL Protocol's ILL_REQUEST message. But while the ILL_REQUEST does a good job of identifying the requested item, it lacks some important information needed to identify the patron placing the request.

In 2001, IPIG members developed a Request Submission Message, intended to provide "a format in which library patrons can electronically submit requests for library material. Use of this standard message format will facilitate the automatic transformation of patrons' requests into protocol-based ILL_REQUESTs when received by ILL Protocol-compliant applications."[13]

The new Request Submission Message defines a comprehensive set of data elements that can accommodate all the needed information, in a standardized format (XML schema) for machine processing. Data elements are grouped into the following categories:

- Client (patron) information
- Bibliographic information
- Possible suppliers
- Request conditions
- Date of request
- System authentication information

The Request Submission Message is not an official addition to the ILL Protocol standard, and thus does not require any formal ballot or approval. The IPIG has published the new message as a draft version for trial use, available for implementation now.

The XML schema and additional information about the message is available at the IPIG web site.[14]

Z39.83–2002 NISO CIRCULATION INTERCHANGE PROTOCOL (NCIP)

NISO's newest standard, NCIP was officially adopted on October 17, 2002. As its name implies, the NCIP standard is a suite of messages designed to carry circulation-related requests and information between systems. NCIP does not define circulation functions or policies, nor does it determine what the user interface to circulation functions should look like. NCIP is based on the standard interchange protocol (SIP) developed by the 3M Corporation for communication between its self-check devices and third-party library management systems.

NCIP is a complex standard, comprising several documents. The Standard as adopted by NISO consists of two documents, *Circulation Interchange Part 1: Protocol (NCIP)* and *Circulation Interchange Part 2: Protocol Implementation Profile 1*.[15] Part 1 includes a description of the NCIP services (message pairs), data elements in each message, and a data dictionary. Part 2 covers the specific technical requirements for implementation using XML. A process has been defined for development of additional implementation profiles, as might be necessitated in the future by changing technology. The current standard also includes two DTDs and XML schemas.

NCIP SERVICES

The NCIP standard defines twenty-five confirmed services, each of which is a pair of messages to be exchanged between systems. Each pair includes an initiation message (a request) and a response. NCIP services are of three types: lookups, updates, and notifications. See Table 4 for a complete list of NCIP services.

Lookup Services are requests from one system for the other system to "tell me what you know" about a user, an item, or an agency (library). The response to a lookup request is the information requested about the specified entity. There is also a lookup service for remote user authentication that asks, "do you recognize and vouch for this user?" with a response of "yes" or "no."

Update Services are requests from one system for the other system to take a specific action. These actions include all the usual circulation ac-

TABLE 4. NCIP Services

Lookup Services
Authenticate User
Lookup Agency
Lookup Item
Lookup User
Lookup Version

Update Services

Accept Item	Renew Item
Check In Item	Report Circulation Status
Check Out Item	Change
Undo Check Out Item	Request Item
Create Agency	Cancel Request Item
Create Item	Send User Notice
Create User	Update Agency
Create User Fiscal	Update Circulation Status
Transaction	Update Item
Recall Item	Update Request Item
Cancel Recall Item	Update User

Notification Services

Agency Created	Item Renewed
Agency Updated	Item Request Cancelled
Circulation Status Change	Item Request Updated
Reported	Item Requested
Circulation Status	Item Shipped
Updated	Item Updated
Item Checked In	User Created
Item Checked Out	User Fiscal Transaction
Item Created	Created
Item Recall Cancelled	User Notice Sent
Item Recalled	User Updated
Item Received	

tivities; for example, the initiating system might ask the responder to check out an item to a user. The circulation transaction will take place in the responder's system, even though the requester initiated it. The response message in an update service is very important; it tells the requester about the result or failure of the requested action. The response to a checkout request might include the due date, or the reason why the item could not be checked out.

Notification Services parallel the Update Services, but here the circulation transaction has already occurred. The initiating system has taken an action and is simply notifying the responder. The responder is not expected to take any action in response to the notification; the response message is simply a confirmation that the notification was received.

APPLICATION AREAS AND PROFILES

NCIP was developed to support three application areas: direct consortial borrowing (DCB), circulation/interlibrary loan interaction (CILL), and self-service circulation (SS). Each of these application areas is described below, along with their supporting draft application profiles.

An application profile describes how NCIP can be used within a particular application domain. The profile describes the application area, identifies all participating applications (systems), defines relevant business rules and indicates which NCIP services must be supported. Application profiles may also require or conditionally require the use of data elements that are optional in the overall standard.

Eight application profiles were prepared as the standard was written, and a process is in place to support the development of additional profiles as needed.[16]

NISO members have not voted on the application profiles, so the profiles as such are not part of the official standard. They were developed concurrently with the standard in hopes of avoiding the kinds of interoperability problems that were common in early Z39.50 implementations. All application profiles are still considered drafts.

Direct Consortial Borrowing (DCB)

Through direct consortial borrowing agreements, users of one library can request and borrow items directly from another library within a consortium. NCIP facilitates the transfer of information about users and items between circulation systems, thereby allowing a library to manage circulation transactions for non-local patrons and/or provide local control of items belonging to another library.

DCB has four draft application profiles, each supporting a different organizational model for consortial borrowing:

- DCB-1: Item Agency Manages Transaction
- DCB-2: User Agency Manages Transaction
- DCB-3: Broker Application Manages Transaction
- DCB-4: User Agency Manages Transactions with Proxy Checkout

Each DCB profile describes messaging between two or more circulation systems. In addition to the user's library (user agency) and the library that owns the requested item (item agency), some profiles include support for item pickup and/or drop-off at a third location, and support for request-brokering agencies.

Circulation/Interlibrary Loan Interaction (CILL)

NCIP facilitates the exchange of circulation data between interlibrary loan systems and circulation systems, permitting libraries to use circulation systems to manage local and interlibrary loans. In this functional area, NCIP is an adjunct to the ILL Protocol that governs the messaging *between* the borrowing and lending libraries. NCIP messaging occurs between the ILL and circulation systems *within* each library.

CILL has two draft application profiles:

- CILL-1: Borrowing Agency
- CILL-2: Lending Agency

Each profile describes messaging between the library's circulation and interlibrary loan management systems. CILL-1 supports the borrowing role, permitting the circulation system to manage all loans to users (locally-owned items as well as items borrowed via ILL). The profile also supports improved physical tracking of ILL items from receipt in the library, transfer to pickup location, checkout by the user, etc. CILL-2 describes interaction between the lending library's circulation and interlibrary loan systems, enabling ILL request status updates and appropriate notices to be sent automatically, and tracking the physical movement of returned items.

Self-Service Circulation (SS)

Self-service applications allow users to check out or check in desired items, and perform a limited range of other circulation-related activities without assistance from library staff.

SS has two draft application profiles:

- SS-1: Unmediated Online Circulation
- SS-2: Unmediated Online Circulation with Offline Recovery

Both profiles describe messaging between a circulation system and a self-service device or web client. Both support check out, check in, renewal, placing holds, and payment of fines and fees, and can support delivery of electronic items. Support is also included for automated check-in/sorter devices. The SS-2 profile includes additional functionality for self-service devices capable of normal operation while offline (i.e., in case of network outage) and uploading transactions to the circulation/server when the connection is restored.

IMPLEMENTATION

Incorporation of NCIP into existing products has begun, but widespread implementation is unlikely until 2004-05. An active implementers' group (NCIP-IG) exists and several pairs of vendors have completed intersystem testing.[17]

How will NCIP be implemented in the marketplace? The developers of the standard originally assumed that application profiles would be implemented in their entirety, but preliminary experience suggests most implementers are taking a different approach. It now appears that the earliest implementations of NCIP will be limited to smaller sets of services–probably those needed to meet current customer demands. Implementation of complete profiles may be several years away.

AUTHOR NOTE

All URLs were verified as of 15 January 2003.

NOTES

1. http://www.loc.gov/z3950/agency/zing/zing-home.html.
2. The Library of Congress is the Z39.50 International Maintenance Agency, http://lcweb.loc.gov/z3950/agency/.

3. Record syntax is a mutually understood data structure and format, e.g., MARC21. Neither system is required to use the specified record syntax for display of results to users.

4. Hodgson, Cynthia. *The RFP Writer's Guide to Standards for Library Systems.* Bethesda, Maryland: NISO Press, 2002. Also available online at http://www. niso.org/standards/resources/RFP_Writers_Guide.pdf.

5. *The Bath Profile: An International Z39.50 Specification for Library Applications and Resource Discovery,* Release 2.0, Draft 3, October 2002. Available online at http://www.nlc-bnc.ca/bath/tp-bath2-e.htm.

6. Lunau, Carrol D. *The Bath Profile: What is it and why should I care?* Ottawa: National Library of Canada, March 15, 2000. Available online at http://www.nlc-bnc. ca/bath/obj/bathfaq.pdf.

7. Librarians often equate the use attribute to the field or index to be searched, but Z39.50 makes no requirements about the fields, data elements or indexes a target must maintain. The documentation states simply: "A use attribute specifies an access point." Z39.50 attributes are not explained in the standard itself, but in a companion document called "bib-1 semantics." The complete reference is *Attribute Set BIB-1 (Z39.50-1995): Semantics.* September 1995, modified October 1997. Available online at ftp://ftp.loc.gov/pub/z3950/defs/bib1.txt.

8. According to bib-1 semantics, "when the origin uses 'any' the intent is that the target locate records via commonly used access points." The Bath Profile indicates that "any" should be interpreted as including at least author, title and subject but targets may also include results from other access points.

9. Profile drafts and other materials may be available at the Committee AV web site, http://www.unt.edu/zprofile/index.html. Once balloted, the U.S. National Profile will be available at http://www.niso.org and http://www.niso.org/standards/resources/Z39-89-200X.pdf.

10. NISO issues some standards as Draft Standards for Trial Use (DSFTU) to allow implementers to test the standard before proceeding to ballot. At the end of the trial period, the standard may be balloted, revised or withdrawn.

11. The National Library of Canada is the ILL Protocol Maintenance Agency, http://www.nlc-bnc.ca/iso/ill/main.htm. The ILL Protocol is not available online.

12. http://www.nlc-bnc.ca/iso/ill/ipd.htm.

13. http://www.nlc-bnc.ca/iso/ill/document/ipigwp/requestsubmissionmessage_1.3. html. In the terminology of the ILL Protocol, a Request is the message sent from a requesting library to a potential supplier. It may therefore be useful to think of the Request Submission Message as "a request for a request."

14. Ibid. The IPIG home page address is http://www.nlc-bnc.ca/iso/ill/implemen.htm.

15. Both of the NCIP documents are available in PDF format at the NISO web site, at http://www.niso.org/standards/resources/z3983pt1rev1.pdf and http://www. niso.org/standards/resources/z3983pt2.pdf. The documents comprising Parts 1 and 2 of the standard are commonly known as "the protocol" and "the implementation profile," respectively.

16. Until a maintenance agency has been designated for NCIP, the draft application profiles are available from NISO, at http://www.niso.org/standards/resources/Z39-83-ApplProfiles.html.

17. NCIP-IG maintains a web site at http://www.lib.uchicago.edu/staffweb/groups/ncip/.

When Terrabytes Meet Terra Firma: Scholarly Information Digitization and Distribution

Thomas Bacher

SUMMARY. As scholarly communication changes, key areas concerning digitization, standards, and cooperation between university libraries and university presses are cornerstones to a better understanding of the future distribution of information. Content issues play a key role in this discussion due to the growth of information avenues, the expansion of subject areas, and the way information can be distributed. In this new digital environment, however, social issues ranging from the feel of books to the outcome of coding options will play a major role in the acceptance of some types of content containers. While clear answers are not yet evident, some future directions can be contemplated. *[Article copies available for a fee from The Haworth Document Delivery Service: 1-800-HAWORTH. E-mail address: <docdelivery@haworthpress.com> Website: <http://www.HaworthPress.com> © 2004 by The Haworth Press, Inc. All rights reserved.]*

KEYWORDS. Digitization, e-book, interdisciplinary, publishing, scholarly communication, university press

Thomas Bacher is Director, Purdue University Press (E-mail: bacher@purdue.edu).

[Haworth co-indexing entry note]: "When Terrabytes Meet Terra Firma: Scholarly Information Digitization and Distribution." Bacher, Thomas. Co-published simultaneously in *Journal of Library Administration* (The Haworth Information Press, an imprint of The Haworth Press, Inc.) Vol. 40, No. 1/2, 2004, pp. 107-126; and: *The Changing Landscape for Electronic Resources: Content, Access, Delivery, and Legal Issues* (ed: Yem S. Fong, and Suzanne M. Ward) The Haworth Information Press, an imprint of The Haworth Press, Inc., 2004, pp. 107-126. Single or multiple copies of this article are available for a fee from The Haworth Document Delivery Service [1-800-HAWORTH, 9:00 a.m. - 5:00 p.m. (EST). E-mail address: docdelivery@haworthpress.com].

Digital Object Identifier: 10.1300/J111v40n01_08

INTRODUCTION

To say that scholarly communication is going through a change underestimates the broad effect of digitization and its outcomes. While content providers, like university presses, initially looked at digital product creation as a panacea and cost-cutting opportunity, digital publishing has not become the mainstay of any university press, let alone any commercial publisher. True, digitization has led to significant advances in online journal distribution, but these trends have found prominence in the sciences and in business where a tradition of shorter-length studies and timely results are key information prerequisites.

Moreover, other factors, especially decreases in subsidies by parent institutions and the impetus to turn university presses into profit centers, have placed an undue burden on important transmitters of scholarly communication. The lack of foresight by university presses, as well as the lack of understanding by university administrators who inadequately funded scholarly publishing operations, allowed commercial publishers to gain significant footholds in scientific content areas, resulting in serious spikes in subscription prices. (See Appendix for a look at cost escalation in library purchases.)

Finally, the growth in niche areas of academic pursuit, coupled with tools that have made it easier to create and distribute content at the faculty level, has brought new players to the table as competitors in the scholarly market (e.g., the Scholarly Publishing and Academic Resources Coalition [SPARC], Bepress, BioMed, PubMed, etc.). Still, the printed book and, to a lesser extent, the printed journal, remain the cornerstones of most scholarly communication, although in the latter case digitization is eroding the reliance on print materials. As important cogs in the scholarly communication wheel, libraries and university presses have a key stake in the outcome of the digital content debate. This article examines several issues in the movement toward reliable, accurate, and dependable digital content with the hopes of steering toward some assumptions for future debate.

A LOOK AT THE CURRENT
SCHOLARLY COMMUNICATION NETWORK

Prior to delving into a discussion of digitization and its effects, a brief look at the scholarly communication network and e-books in particular provides a framework for the subsequent dialogue. Figure 1 presents a simplified look at scholarly communication stakeholders.

FIGURE 1. Current Scholarly Communication Network

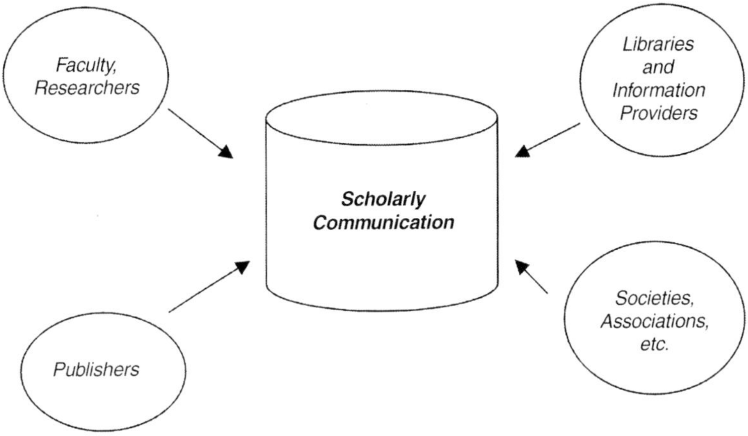

As expected, these entities have a great impact on the type and format of information that flows through the system. Faculty and researchers create or assimilate segments of information and influence the format of information through tenure and other professional requirements. Publishers, including and university and commercial presses, influence information selection through editorial processes, and determine the format of information through return-on-investment and other financial requirements. University libraries and other information databanks influence information selection by collecting in specific subject areas and by determining the amount and format of information according to their budgets. Most professional societies and associations function both as creators of information resources and as publishers.

Figure 2 shows the typical flow of scholarly information starting with the information creator, usually faculty or researchers at a think tank or institution of higher learning. This information is manipulated (edited, formatted, marketed, etc.) by another organization, a not-for-profit or commercial press, and developed into one of many end-products. The information is then purchased by an individual or by a larger information databank, typically a university library. Finally, the use of this newly released information spawns further research and product development.

The macro-impact of scholarly information weighs on universities in several cost areas: (1) the salaries of faculty and researchers; (2) library budgets; and (3) subsidies to university presses. All participants feel the

FIGURE 2. The Flow of Information

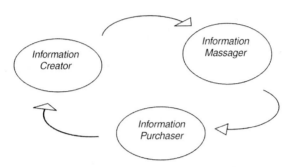

economic pressures on the communication system because of the higher than expected (above inflation) cost increases in science, technical and medical (STM) journals, the steady increase in monograph pricing, and the academic "publish or perish" mentality.

Under the current system, universities pay twice (if not three times when university presses are factored in) for the information; once when the content is created and again when it is purchased. Further, universities with presses subsidize the entire system of global scholarship. University presses do not charge higher amounts for their titles to university libraries at institutions without university presses, and universities with university presses buy publications that aid the tenure process at non-university-press institutions.

Finally, the proliferation of information and the speed at which it comes to market continues to increase. The need for early and well-directed digitization programs and rights management systems is becoming more apparent in today's information economy. The need is both internal and external. On the one hand, an early system of collection and formatting provides a databank through which university departments share ongoing research findings. On the other hand, as data in the internal system are vetted and substantiated, they can be shared across universities. In this way, universities will be able to maximize their investment in scholarly information because over time commercial publishers will become less prominent as information providers.

A LITTLE E-BOOK GOES A LONG WAY

Consider e-books. Although definitions can be misleading, an e-book can be simply defined as a digitized content compendium that goes through some translator package and is viewable on some device. In most cases, the e-book tries to replicate a printed book and its objects: table of content, chapters, pages, an index, and so on. Perceptions are more important than definitions, but most people would say that the traditional book is not an e-book.

However, most e-books in the digital marketplace are not pure in the sense that they are simply digital copies that were produced along a traditional production path whose primary end product was still a printed book. This add-on e-book does not substantially alter expenses especially if a standard digital container is chosen, e.g., PDF or Lit files. Conversion costs range between $50 and $500 depending on the number and type of conversions desired. Recent data indicate that although initial forecasts of stellar growth in the e-book market were misguided, some e-book market segments have grown respectably. For example, Palm Digital Media reports that nearly 180,000 e-books were sold in 2001. For comparison, about 60,000 books were published in the United States in 2000 (http://aaupnet.org/news/glance.html). This figure represents an increase of more than 40% from 2000. In July 2002, McGraw-Hill Professional e-book sales were up 55% over the same period of the previous year (from the Open ebook Forum website: www.openebook.org).

An additional factor in the slower than expected growth in the e-book market, other than weak demand, is the advent of very short-run printing alternatives that have lowered the per unit cost of titles. One hundred print copy runs with as few as twenty-five copy reprint runs are not uncommon since they fill the information needs in some niche professional and scholarly markets. Overhead and editorial costs have to be worked into this model, but these costs would not have evaporated by creating a digital-only monographic edition (Day, 1998).

Overdorf and Barragree examine how disruptive new technologies, like e-books, tend to be absorbed into traditional product development paths under good management practices. While well-intentioned, this practice leads to disaster. "A disruptive technology, in contrast [to sustaining technologies that enhance current products], will not appeal to an established firm's current customers, because it typically promises worse performance according to metrics that existing customers value" (Overdorf and Barragee, p. 4). Since performance-based review systems usually look at short-term (annual) performance, managers tend to eliminate risk for the comfort of current products. Also, larger corporate entities can actually absorb new technologies, if necessary, through acquisitions that allow smaller organizations to become risk takers in the first place.

Faulty business judgments also forced market categorizations that were unsuited to e-books. E-books were marketed as a convenience for the traditional book buyer. An e-book, viewed as a replica of the printed book, promised instant availability. With an Internet connection, potential buyers could be anywhere in the world and find content that they wanted. However, the e-book was a different product with different traits that required adaptations by the end-user. Unfortunately, many publishers needed to fit the technology, if they were to market it at all, into an existing pattern of feedback from their current customers. Many early e-book initiatives were quickly sent to the scrap heap.

Recently, a significant restructuring in the e-book vendor market (the netLibrary case, for example) has occurred. Investments in e-books and other compendiums of digital content, however, will become more common over the next decade. Projects like the American Council of Learned Societies (ACLS) History Project, initiatives similar to the Committee on Institutional Cooperation (CIC) Electronic Publishing Venture, and destination web presences such as Columbia International Affairs Online (CIAO) will find more support.

Still, the lack of any predominant digital distribution system makes the business modeling process very difficult for information providers. Many organizations collect content but only distribute that content in ways that provide returns on investment. The outlook for higher education funding is not bright for the next several years and this will have a deleterious effect on new, untested ventures including monograph data basing (basically XML-coding of monographic content that can be readily and deeply searchable) and content distribution. However, the Gartner Group sees a move toward less sophisticated web content management systems like Atomz, iUpload, and Clickability because organizations have discovered that customers are not demanding bells and whistles and that the costs for the systems have dropped dramatically. In the digital rights area, the Gartner Group predicts that high-value content sectors, including books, will continue to experience falling revenues and, unfortunately, business-to-consumer initiatives will do more harm than good (Gilbert et al., 2002).

THE CONTENT STORY

Is It One for the Money or Is It Two for the Show?

On a beautiful fall day in 1984, employees of the American Branch, as well as several key members of the home office management team,

gathered on the second floor of the New York Public Library to cele-
brate the 400th anniversary of the Cambridge University Press, the old-
est continually operating university press in the world. Speeches were
given espousing the continuity that the Press had brought to scholarship
by publishing works by John Milton, Isaac Newton, Richard P.
Feynman, and Richard Rorty. The Press traced its origins to a royal
charter granted to Cambridge University by Henry VII in which he

> . . . by the grace of God, King of England and France, Defender of
> the Faith, and Lord of Ireland . . . have granted and given licence,
> and by these presents grant and give licence, for ourselves and our
> heirs, to our beloved in Christ the Chancellor, Masters and
> Scholars of our University of Cambridge . . . from time to time as-
> sign, appoint and in perpetuity have among them, and perpetually
> remaining and dwelling within our aforesaid University, Three
> Stationers and Printers or Sellers of Books . . . and also to exhibit
> for sale, as well in the same University as elsewhere in our realm,
> wherever they please, all such books and all other books wherever
> printed, both within and outside our realm. (McKitterick, 1992)

In the early years, the scope of university press publishing was quite
limited. Oxford University Press, one year younger than Cambridge,
was primarily a Bible publisher until the twentieth century. As presses
developed and as fields of study expanded, university press publications also diversified. Harvard University Press's third director, Dumas
Malone, saw the Press's mission as the publication of "'scholarship
plus,' that is, not merely highly specialized works, but works for the
general intellectual reader" (from the Harvard University Press website,
www.hup.harvard.edu). This dual role has remained at the heart of most
university presses' publishing programs. Johns Hopkins's current mission clearly indicates the direction of most university presses' publishing programs. "Our primary mission is to seek out and publish books
and journals of superior quality that contribute significantly to the progress of research and learning. Also vital to our mission is publication for
a broader community, including students, who use our books and journals in their studies; professionals, who consult them to keep abreast of
rapidly changing fields; and general readers, who find in them enjoy-
ment as well as enlightenment" (from the Johns Hopkins University
Press website, www.press.jhu.edu/press).

The tension presses face between the niche and the general environment has proved difficult to manage. Many acquisition editors tell of

query letters stating that while a topic area might have a small intellectual constituency, the proposed book will be of interest to the general reader, too. Astute editors usually dismiss this nonsense. Further, only larger university presses enjoy the marketing and publicity clout to penetrate the distribution channels necessary for maximum exposure and the subsequent "word of mouth advertising" that is the prerequisite for a bestseller. In this regard, there is little use in comparing a Purdue University Press with a Cambridge University Press because the economics of size and the breadth of resources are clearly in Cambridge's favor.

When commercial presses chose to give up on some mid-list titles in the 1990s, some university presses saw a potential opportunity to increase revenues. However, the foray into uncharted distribution channels resulted in higher costs. Many presses currently back away from these ventures, concentrating on their fundamental role as distributors of scholarship. The overblown publicity that a press generates when it publishes a bestseller, like Tom Clancy's *The Hunt for Red October* for the Naval Institute Press, can blind administrators to the true mission of a press not to mention the sheer luck of finding such authors.

Is There a Free Information Lunch or Are We Headed for Horn & Hardart's?

Through early years spent in the publishing industry in New York City, the author personally experienced the last Horn & Hardart's Automat before the ingenious institution finally gave way to McDonald's and other fast-food joints. The unique feature of H&H was that it was filled with walls full of coin-operated food vending choices. Customers dropped in coins for a sandwich; more coins for a piece of pie, or a drink, or a side-dish. The choices were completely individual. It was pay as you go.

Content digitization, with its ease of slicing and dicing, is ready to become a full-choice, piecemeal business. What reemerges is the primacy for publishers or other information manipulators to collect and copyright crucial content since the distribution mechanism, over time, will be less significant. Information vending will not be concerned with the size of the end product since e-commerce systems will be able to price content from tidbits to tomes. Collecting and copyrighting content will become even more valuable than previously. Also, the collection might be divorced from a product. While a book might be created from some of a publisher's content, the publisher might also collect other results from a researcher for web-only distribution.

As universities realize the value in the heritage of their own instruction and research that fosters intra-disciplinary exchange, administrators will appreciate the university press's mature distribution network, editorial know-how, and content handling abilities. In the quest for technology answers, administrators must shy away from letting technologists alone provide solutions to academic problems. While technology provides digital rights management systems, for example, technology cannot determine if information is worth managing in the first place. One subtle and overlooked value of university presses is their long history of working with faculty and librarians to meet information needs.

Rousseau was famous for his quote that "man is born free, and everywhere he is in chains" (Rousseau, 1968). As the Internet has provided the structure for expanding the breadth of information (largely unverified), and as sources of real-time information have expanded, Rousseau's quote might be reworked to reflect that information is created freely, and everywhere it is owned by someone else. Obviously, there is a cost for information creation, but Internet users have come to expect that vast amounts of information should be free. After all, technology created a whole new lending phenomenon with the advent of Napster. Although the music industry was successful in stopping Napster, song lending and duplication continues and CD sales decline. Apple is now selling songs for 99 cents each.

More information is now available on how researchers actually go about collecting digital data. This information verifies that a clear trend exists, especially for young researchers. The academics will "go around subscription barriers (both for paper and electronic materials) and rely almost exclusively on what they can find free on the Internet, which often includes working versions posted on home pages of the authors" (Björk, 2000).

Overwrought or Oversought

The expansion and specialization of subject areas over the last twenty years have led to an escalation in the number of publications, some of which interest only a handful of researchers. This is most evident in the sciences, an area that commercial publishers identified early as a significant growth area. However, extending "scholarly publishing to commercial publishers also meant that authors turned over the rights to their works, hence sowing the seeds for the current crisis" of spiraling journal costs that were 10-15% above the consumer price index (Lawal, 2001). One suggested solution is that faculty members could become self-publishers and bypass traditional means for distribution by using the Internet. But in an age when researchers also experience information overload, placing the extra burden of self-publication on them will lessen their teaching and laboratory explorations.

Silos of research, evident in the many narrowly-focused investigative university nodes, strain university budgets. Government sponsored research programs provide many grants for the sciences, but the humanities and arts divvy up a much smaller pie. The primacy of science and business, where the technology revolution has taken place, made a rounded education less desirable to both students and administrators. Table 1 depicts master's degrees awarded by field of study from 1970-71 through 1999-2000. Indexed to the 1970-71 total degrees, the evidence is clear. The greatest percentage rise over this period has been in areas like computer and information sciences, health professions and related sciences, and business.

Interestingly, while some areas, like education, have declined significantly, the raw numbers have still increased, except in areas that are the traditional strength of university press publishing programs: philosophy and religion, social sciences and history, and English language and literature. While university presses complained that libraries were buying fewer monographs, libraries were in fact purchasing materials to support the rapid growth areas of their institutions' educational programs. Even if a university press wanted to shift disciplinary focus, backlogs of traditional titles already in the pipeline delayed changes.

In today's academic environment, we see a greater move toward interdisciplinary education. Obviously, research findings in the vacuum of departmental silos not only created philosophical and ethical problems, but also failed to maximize discoveries. Unlike in the past, "the projects, not the disciplines, define the terms of engagement. The relationship between science and engineering, for example, is no longer summarized in a set of reliable equations; it now includes all the complexities of evolving life forms" (Williams, 2003). Further, in some areas of scholarship the growth of technology fostered publishing opportunities. Researchers in disciplines that are media- or audio-intensive can now communicate in a much richer way. Small organizations, like the Society for Seventeenth-Century Music, whose membership numbers are a deterrent to a print publication, have a digital avenue for the exchange of ideas. As one researcher notes, while paper is "wonderful for holding and reading text . . . paper cannot sing" (Snyder, 2001).

TABLE 1. Master's Degree Conferred by Field of Study as Percentage of Total Master's Degrees Conferred*

Field of study	1970-71	Number of Degrees	1999-2000	Number of Degrees	Indexed to 1971	% Change
Parks, recreation, leisure and fitness studies	0.001	218	0.005	2478	1250	473%
Transportation and material moving workers	0.000	63	0.002	697	352	458%
Computer and information sciences	0.007	1588	0.031	14264	7194	353%
Health professions and related sciences	0.025	5749	0.093	42456	21412	272%
Engineering-related technologies	0.001	134	0.002	926	467	249%
Communications technologies	0.000	86	0.001	436	220	156%
Business	0.113	25977	0.246	112258	56616	118%
Law and legal studies	0.004	955	0.008	3750	1891	98%
Multi/interdisciplinary studies	0.004	821	0.007	3064	1545	88%
Public administration and services	0.034	7785	0.056	25594	12908	66%
Communications	0.008	1770	0.011	5169	2607	47%
Psychology	0.025	5717	0.032	14465	7295	28%
Architecture and related programs	0.007	1705	0.009	4268	2152	26%
Theological studies/religious vocations	0.012	2710	0.012	5576	2812	4%
Home economics and vocational home economics	0.006	1452	0.006	2830	1427	−2%
Agriculture and natural resources	0.011	2457	0.010	4375	2206	−10%
Visual and performing arts	0.029	6675	0.024	10918	5506	−18%
Engineering	0.071	16309	0.056	25596	12909	−21%
Area, ethnic, and cultural studies	0.004	1032	0.003	1591	802	−22%
Education	0.380	87666	0.272	124240	62658	−29%
Biological sciences/life sciences	0.025	5728	0.014	6198	3126	−45%
Philosophy and religion	0.006	1326	0.003	1329	670	−49%
Social sciences and history	0.072	16539	0.031	14066	7094	−57%
Physical sciences and science technologies	0.028	6367	0.011	4841	2441	−62%
English language and literature/letters	0.046	10686	0.016	7230	3646	−66%
Library science	0.030	7001	0.010	4577	2308	−67%

TABLE 1 (continued)

Field of study	1970-71	Number of Degrees	1999-2000	Number of Degrees	Indexed to 1971	% Change
Mathematics	0.025	5695	0.007	3412	1721	−70%
Foreign languages and literatures	0.023	5217	0.006	2780	1402	−73%
Other	0.005	1081	0.017	7672	3869	258%

*230,509 master's degrees were conferred in 1970-71 and 457,056 master's degrees were conferred in 1999-2000.

NOTE: The new Classification of Instructional Programs was initiated in 1991-92. The figures for earlier years have been reclassified when necessary to make them conform to the new taxonomy. To facilitate trend comparisons, certain aggregations have been made of the degree fields as reported in the IPEDS

"Completions" survey: "Agriculture and natural resources" includes Agricultural business and production, Agricultural sciences, and Conservation and renewable natural resources; "Business" includes Business management and administrative services, Marketing operations/marketing and distribution, and Consumer and personal services; and "Engineering-related technologies" includes Engineering-related technologies, Mechanics and repairers, and Construction trades.

Data for 1998-99 imputed using alternative procedures.

SOURCE: U.S. Department of Education, National Center for Education Statistics, Higher Education General Information Survey (HEGIS), "Degrees and Other Formal Awards Conferred" surveys, and Integrated Postsecondary Education Data System (IPEDS), "Completions" surveys. (This table was prepared August 2001.)

These particular calculations and indexing of material performed by the author.

THE SOCIAL STORY

Collaboration or Confusion

Recently, at the author's first grader's birthday party, the guests particularly enjoyed the telephone game. An adult tells one child a phrase and that child whispers the phrase to another. The game continues until the last child has heard the phrase and says it out loud. Invariably, the phrase has changed from beginning to end. Does the same distortion occur when digitizing what was formerly printed information? Since the digitization of content is a relatively new process, investigations into the social ramifications of digitization are also new.

As Russell (2001) notes, both informal and formal "communications are undergoing radical alterations such that the distinction between the two is becoming increasingly blurred. This paling of established divisions is a key element in the shift from print to electronic media . . . affecting not only the way information is being exchanged but also the institutions responsible for information processing and provision." We have seen this especially in the many "pseudo-publishing" organizations that have appeared over the last decade. Advances in text formatting software have allowed more entities and individuals the power to publish. The Internet has given the masses the power to distribute. However, as professional information gatekeepers know, the abundance of information does not mean that all information meets scholarly standards. When computers were first introduced, a descriptive adage also became commonplace to describe the verifiability of results: Garbage in, garbage out. This maxim also applies in the nascent digital environment.

Even if less-established publishing entities can ensure that their content is sound, sometimes not all costs in the process are readily seen. For example, the SPARC initiative, while well-intentioned, simply shifts financial burdens to libraries and researchers. Members pay up to $12,000 to support a program to create less-expensive alternatives to existing high-cost commercial journals (see the SPARC membership page on the Association of Research Libraries [ARL] website: www.arl.org). Publishing personnel costs for editing and typesetting are now being replaced by faculty time costs and/or library personnel costs. Indeed, a bureaucracy to manage SPARC has grown up around the idea of saving costs.

While it is clear that functions cannot be replaced along the scholarly publishing process, further questions need to be raised about the longevity and sustainability of projects like SPARC. In good economic times, funding is more prevalent for ideas that generally provide the promise of cost savings for an academic institution. However, as finances become constrained, membership fees and other non-essential programs can be affected dramatically. While market forces, funding issues, and the like have influenced scholarly publishing for decades, university presses have a record of longevity, consistency, and authority that newer information distribution programs do not. The mirage that somehow paints scholarly publishing with a coat of no-cost primer does a disservice to the entire endeavor.

In addition, researchers and faculty members are themselves hindrances to digital programs and online journals. Because of tenure issues, scholars need to make sure that their work appears in visible and prestigious publications, no matter if these publications have digital editions. Pressures on library budgets compound the problem. As serials reduction programs continue to eliminate publications, visibility means that a publication is available on the researcher's campus. Librarians answer to their constituencies by buying what is most needed, in total, by their faculty. Thus, the demand for particular publications rises significantly over time as less popular publications are not renewed.

WYSIWYG or WYSInotWYG

An article in *The Chronicle of Higher Education* noted that the "very differences between digital forms of expression, on the one hand, and alphanumeric and graphical forms we are accustomed to from books, on the other hand, give us a remarkable vantage from which to study books and paper works in which so much of our cultural heritage is stored for us" (McGann, 2002). As we digitize materials, we adjust relationships between the materials in a way that mirrors quantum fields. New information is created as new relationships among formalized structures (SGML/XML) are created. In a word, informational reality is a set of points in space at a given time. The stability of a document is thus user driven through a search mechanism. McGann's concern is that we do not have "people well trained in the theory and practice of scholarly method and editing," which could lead to incorrect mark-up and subsequent content confusion. While a book presents a whole, digitization can in fact create parts that do not add up to that whole.

XML mark-up deconstructs information and then recombines it to provide personalized contents for particular individuals. Thus, coding decisions become critical and require a good editing sense as well as a good knowledge of particular subject content. Special organizations, like university presses, that have high editorial standards and the staff to carry out such projects, will need to play a key role in the rules subsets that go along with the coding.

The act of coding content points out an underlying concern that many have voiced about digital information. While a book provides a tactile copy of research that can be kept and referred to in its original state, digital content makes changeability much more of an issue. Which version of a particular article, like this one, is the penultimate version? How can we save website content so that citations are still relevant a year from now? Digitization provides an answer to archiving issues, but digitization is also the devil in disguise because information variability brings a new set of issues to the librarian's table already overpopulated with printed content.

In many cases, too, organizations are only licensing rights to view online content. Ownership used to lie in the hands of people and organizations that purchased materials. Under the new digital rules, content that was available one day might be restricted the next. Also, online delivery puts a real burden on information networks. As researchers continue to use digital content and to retrieve materials rapidly, any network degradation is noticed immediately. Downtime closes everyone's library.

Wide-Open Spaces or Controllable Places

Bousquet contends that the informatics of higher education poses some key threats to continuous information flow. Informatics, the "managerial logic through which university administrators have transformed the academic workplace on the model of information, so that education (and the labor providing it) is increasingly 'delivered' as data, flowing in a bitstream highly responsive to managerial direction" (Bousquet, 2002) has led to just-in-time deployment of resources, especially faculty themselves, and to the overuse of graduate students and full-time instructors not tied to a tenure path. If the trend continues, full-time, tenured faculty positions will decline and the numbers of "migrant" lecturers and instructors will increase. Universities will have to face the possibility of maintaining a steady and easily rewriteable instructional legacy.

University prestige is directly affected by its intellectual legacy. The Harvards and Stanfords and Cornells of the world pass a legacy from one generation to the next. Even as technology provides us the benefit of collecting this legacy, we are not suited to do so. If Bousquet is correct, we will see a loss of academic advancement. While we concentrate on delivering information to the desktop, expand ways to provide distance education, and figure out what role multimedia plays in the classroom, our information systems are not designed to archive instructional copy, lectures, class notes, reading lists, etc. Much of the creativity and discovery at universities is at the teaching faculty and student level. When a prominent educator leaves a teaching position, much of the subtle information of his or her work goes away, too. The process of learning is subordinated to a final outcome.

CONCLUSIONS

As digitization provides greater access to information and as the information becomes more reliable, two heads or four heads or six heads will be better than one. It is clear that the Internet has opened many paths to better discovery, aiding in "supporting faculty productivity, especially in the stimulation and refinement of ideas among scholars" (Henry, 2002). While face-to-face meetings yield a great deal and allow for very concerted efforts to iron out differences and create newer paths

for advancement, e-mail exchanges tend to be more vibrant and vitri-
olic. Moreover, scholars from the far reaches of the world can meet virtually. Many areas of scholarship, especially in the sciences, have
developed as rapidly as communication has allowed. Cultural differences encourage better results because the diversity of researchers
brings different assumptions to a situation.

Koenig notes that open communication must be balanced against the
valuation of information as intellectual capital. In the information age,
ideas and findings are the currency of the realm and must be guarded as
such. However, "to create further intellectual capital, to put new intellectual capital into the pipeline, requires openness and accessibility,
both in and out, to a rich information and communication environment"
(Koenig, 2001). Organizations with easily accessible information tend
to generate better ideas that result in better outcomes. In studying pharmaceutical organizations, Koenig found that "the greater the emphasis
upon protecting the company's proprietary data, the less successful the
company was in terms of creating new pharmaceutical products and
getting new products into the pipeline." He also observed that productivity was self fulfilling. That is, an open information flow, in which
codification of information represents only 50% of all data, encouraged
researchers to use their corporate library more often and to use it much
more for "browsing and keeping abreast, as opposed to using it to address a specific information need."

While heeding Koenig's concern about over-codification, some rules
need to be put into place to define schemes for scholarly information
gathering. An organization like the Association of American University
Presses (AAUP) could play a vital role in this process, but it does not
seem willing. Instead, over the last decade organizations of librarians
have taken the lead in this area and the visibility has aided their cause
with home administrators. In many ways university presses are seen as
entities that are hindering progress by hoping to resurrect the past.

"Eventually, the difference between a university publisher and a university librarian will become quite insignificant . . . in the future the university presses will need to work more closely with libraries, and it is
not to soon to start" (Berry, 1987). A former director of Princeton University Press, Herbert Bailey, made these remarks at the 50th anniversary meeting of the AAUP in 1987. In 2003, evidence of the lack of
communication has led to the advent of the library as publisher. In the
next five years, universities themselves could create a channel on the
new Internet specifically designed to share scholarly information. Under such a scenario, university publishing will become predominantly

internal, making university presses the formatters of information and university libraries the distributors of information, bypassing commercial scholarly publishers altogether. Of course, this scenario would require a commitment by administrators to fund such an endeavor, but costs could truly be shared across institutions and could be controlled in a way that is not currently possible.

One of Bob Dylan's lyrics expounds an interesting philosophy, "If you ain't got nothing, you got nothing to lose." The counterargument, of course, is that if you have something (content), you have everything (market) to lose. The crux of the current crisis in scholarly communication revolves around this notion. Economically, the perception of what the future holds determines today's actions. In the scholarly information arena today, players enforce strict controls over content and buy up competitors to form a near monopoly of certain content. Another lyric by the Rolling Stones says bluntly: "You can't always get what you want. But, if you try sometime. You just might find. You get what you need." So, if there is nothing to lose, what will we get?

In any future discussion of scholarly communication and publishing, several issues need to be discussed and resolved. Faculty and researchers are willing to give up their copyright in limited ways to ensure that their work is published in a respected journal or published by a reputable organization. The form of the final product is not of concern to this group as long as tenure rules are relaxed to encompass digital content in the same way that print content is currently viewed. Faculty and researchers would like to have their content available to a community of like scholars and be able to use that content within their universities, for teaching purposes perhaps, through a mechanism that does not solely rely on distributing the material through approved sources or paying extra fees.

Libraries want to find ways to contain costs for needed research materials and to make more materials available if possible. Archiving issues are making digital storage more appealing, but standards questions still abound. As entities, libraries have found many ways to cooperate and have had to upgrade their technological infrastructures. This feature, along with their interlibrary loan and document distribution capabilities, has set the groundwork for a future in which libraries may play the roles of information aggregators and distributors for their parent institutions.

Universities will want to increase their return on investment in their faculty by creating both knowledge management and rights management systems. As technology affords easier and more defined ways to collect intra-university content, more administrators will see the savings in this practice. In this way, universities will be able to maintain a record of the process of learning, too. The process will inform new faculty and aid students in their academic progress.

Publishers, especially commercial entities, will either have to work more closely with university libraries or show true cost structures and price their products accordingly. If they fail to do so, a smaller stream of scholarly content will be available to them. University presses will become more adept at working together with libraries to create subject-specific, digital content compendiums. University presses will also become the editorial engines that gather intra-university content in a way that makes the content easily available for distribution in many different containers.

One of the questions job interviewers traditionally ask is "what do you expect to be doing in five years?" That question was appropriate in a less technology-driven world. Now the question should be "what do you expect to be doing next month?" University libraries and university presses may not know all the answers, but without a concerted effort to cooperate in the area of scholarly communication, the best solution will be found outside the university environment.

NOTES

Berry III, John N. 1987. "A New Alliance Aborning?" *Library Journal,* 112 (August): 56-60.

Björk, Bo-Christer and Turk, Ziga. 2002. "How Scientists Retrieve Publications: An Empirical Study of How the Internet Is Overtaking Paper Media." *The Journal of Electronic Publishing* 6 (2), www.press.umich.edu/jep/06-02/bjork.html.

Bousquet, Marc. 2002. "The Informal and the Informational." *Workplace* 5 (1), www.louisville.edu/journal/workplace/issue5p1/bousquetinformal.html.

Day, Colin. 1998. "Digital Alternatives: Solving the Problem or Shifting the Cost?" *The Journal of Electronic Publishing* 4 (1), www.press.umich.edu/jep/04-01/day.html.

Gilbert, Mark, Logan, Debra, and Shegda, Karen. "Seven Areas of Content Management Growth for 2003." *The Garnter Group,* December 2002, Com-18-6161.

Henry, Paul D. 2002. "Scholarly Use of the Internet by Faculty Members: Factors and Outcomes of Change." *Journal of Research on Technology in Education* 35 (1):49-57.

Koenig, Michael E. D. 2001. "Lessons from the Study of Scholarly Communication for the New Information Era." *Scientometrics 51(3):*511-523.

Lawal, Ibironke. 2001. "Scholarly Communication at the Turn of the Millennium: A Bibliographic Essay." *Journal of Scholarly Publishing* 32 (3):136-154.

McGann, Jerome J. "Literary Scholarship in the Digital Future." *The Chronicle of Higher Education: The Chronicle Review* December 13, 2002, pp. B7-B9.

McKitterick, David. 1992. *A History of Cambridge University Press: Volume 1.* Cambridge University Press.

Overdorf, Michael and Barragee, Amy. 2001. "The Impending Disruption of the Publishing Industry." *Publishing Research Quarterly*, 16 (Fall):3-18.

Rousseau, Jean-Jacques. 1968. *The Social Contract*. Baltimore: Pelican-Penguin: 49.

Russell, Jane M. 2001. "Scientific Communication at the Beginning of the Twenty-First Century." *International Social Science Journal* 53(168):271-282.

Snyder, Kerala J. 2001. "Electronic Journals and the Future of Scholarly Communication." *Notes* 58(1):34-38.

Williams, Rosalind. "Education for the Profession Formerly Known as Engineering." *The Chronicle of Higher Education: The Chronicle Review*, January 24, 2003: B12-B13.

APPENDIX

Monograph and Serial Costs in ARL Libraries, 1986-2002 Median Values for Time-Series Trends						
Year	Serial Unit Cost	Serial Expenditures	Monograph Unit Cost	Monograph Expenditures	Serials Purchased	Monographs Purchased
No. of Libraries	(38)	(103)	(61)	(99)	(38)	(61)
1986	$88.55	$1,517,724	$28.70	$1,120,645	16,173	32,425
1987	$105.48	$1,770,567	$31.81	$1,064,484	16,601	26,204
1988	$116.65	$1,979,604	$36.03	$1,141,226	16,254	25,529
1989	$128.59	$2,130,162	$38.43	$1,241,133	16,298	26,997
1990	$132.45	$2,304,744	$40.41	$1,330,747	16,221	27,545
1991	$153.46	$2,578,309	$42.29	$1,400,738	16,251	27,388
1992	$168.20	$2,630,827	$43.76	$1,353,865	15,896	25,953
1993	$186.50	$2,919,756	$43.74	$1,295,807	15,668	24,933
1994	$195.99	$2,932,091	$44.29	$1,309,807	15,698	25,321
1995	$213.05	$3,133,885	$44.98	$1,365,575	14,741	25,695
1996	$221.17	$3,393,307	$46.73	$1,444,015	15,223	25,560
1997	$244.33	$3,674,368	$46.42	$1,460,234	15,450	28,494
1998	$244.88	$3,818,832	$47.59	$1,486,764	15,166	24,133
1999	$269.90	$4,098,075	$47.05	$1,506,651	15,260	24,311
2000	$301.09	$4,431,593	$47.59	$1,657,349	15,223	27,243
2001	$279.07	$4,710,371	$48.09	$1,864,023	15,342	29,518
2002	$289.84	$4,963,111	$50.17	$1,812,826	17,676	30,752
Avg. Annual % Change	7.7%	7.7%	3.6%	3.1%	0.6%	−0.3%

Source: *ARL Statistics 2001-2002*, Association of Resource Libraries, Washington, DC.

Index

The Dynamic Library Organizations in a Changing Environment, edited by Joan Giesecke, MLS, DPA (Vol. 20, No. 2, 1995). *"Provides a significant look at potential changes in the library world and presents its readers with possible ways to address the negative results of such changes. . . . Covers the key issues facing today's libraries . . . Two thumbs up!" (Marketing Library Resources)*

Access, Ownership, and Resource Sharing, edited by Sul H. Lee (Vol. 20, No. 1, 1995). *The contributing authors present a useful and informative look at the current status of information provision and some of the challenges the subject presents.*

Libraries as User-Centered Organizations: Imperatives for Organizational Change, edited by Meredith A. Butler (Vol. 19, No. 3/4, 1994). *"Presents a very timely and well-organized discussion of major trends and influences causing organizational changes." (Science Books & Films)*

Declining Acquisitions Budgets: Allocation, Collection Development and Impact Communication, edited by Sul H. Lee (Vol. 19, No. 2, 1994). *"Expert and provocative. . . . Presents many ways of looking at library budget deterioration and responses to it . . . There is much food for thought here." (Library Resources & Technical Services)*

The Role and Future of Special Collections in Research Libraries: British and American Perspectives, edited by Sul H. Lee (Vol. 19, No. 1, 1993). *"A provocative but informative read for library users, academic administrators, and private sponsors." (International Journal of Information and Library Research)*

Catalysts for Change: Managing Libraries in the 1990s, edited by Gisela M. von Dran, DPA, MLS, and Jennifer Cargill, MSLS, MSEd (Vol. 18, No. 3/4, 1994). *"A useful collection of articles which focuses on the need for librarians to employ enlightened management practices in order to adapt to and thrive in the rapidly changing information environment." (Australian Library Review)*

Integrating Total Quality Management in a Library Setting, edited by Susan Jurow, MLS, and Susan B. Barnard, MLS (Vol. 18, No. 1/2, 1993). *"Especially valuable are the librarian experiences that directly relate to real concerns about TQM. Recommended for all professional reading collections." (Library Journal)*

Leadership in Academic Libraries: Proceedings of the W. Porter Kellam Conference, The University of Georgia, May 7, 1991, edited by William Gray Potter (Vol. 17, No. 4, 1993). *"Will be of interest to those concerned with the history of American academic libraries." (Australian Library Review)*

Collection Assessment and Acquisitions Budgets, edited by Sul H. Lee (Vol. 17, No. 2, 1993). *Contains timely information about the assessment of academic library collections and the relationship of collection assessment to acquisition budgets.*

Developing Library Staff for the 21st Century, edited by Maureen Sullivan (Vol. 17, No. 1, 1992). *"I found myself enthralled with this highly readable publication. It is one of those rare compilations that manages to successfully integrate current general management operational thinking in the context of academic library management." (Bimonthly Review of Law Books)*

Vendor Evaluation and Acquisition Budgets, edited by Sul H. Lee (Vol. 16, No. 3, 1992). *"The title doesn't do justice to the true scope of this excellent collection of papers delivered at the sixth annual conference on library acquisitions sponsored by the University of Oklahoma Libraries." (Kent K. Hendrickson, BS, MALS, Dean of Libraries, University of Nebraska-Lincoln) Find insightful discussions on the impact of rising costs on library budgets and management in this groundbreaking book.*

The Management of Library and Information Studies Education, edited by Herman L. Totten, PhD, MLS (Vol. 16, No. 1/2, 1992). *"Offers something of interest to everyone connected with LIS education–the undergraduate contemplating a master's degree, the doctoral student struggling with courses and career choices, the new faculty member aghast at conflicting responsibilities, the experienced but stressed LIS professor, and directors of LIS Schools." (Education Libraries)*

Library Management in the Information Technology Environment: Issues, Policies, and Practice for Administrators, edited by Brice G. Hobrock, PhD, MLS (Vol. 15, No. 3/4, 1992). *"A road map to identify some of the alternative routes to the electronic library." (Stephen Rollins, Associate Dean for Library Services, General Library, University of New Mexico)*

Managing Technical Services in the 90's, edited by Drew Racine (Vol. 15, No. 1/2, 1991). *"Presents an eclectic overview of the challenges currently facing all library technical services efforts. . . . Recommended to library administrators and interested practitioners." (Library Journal)*

Budgets for Acquisitions: Strategies for Serials, Monographs, and Electronic Formats, edited by Sul H. Lee (Vol. 14, No. 3, 1991). *"Much more than a series of handy tips for the careful shopper. This [book] is a most useful one–well-informed, thought-provoking, and authoritative." (Australian Library Review)*

Creative Planning for Library Administration: Leadership for the Future, edited by Kent Hendrickson, MALS (Vol. 14, No. 2, 1991). *"Provides some essential information on the planning process, and the mix of opinions and methodologies, as well as examples relevant to every library manager, resulting in a very readable foray into a topic too long avoided by many of us." (Canadian Library Journal)*

Strategic Planning in Higher Education: Implementing New Roles for the Academic Library, edited by James F. Williams, II, MLS (Vol. 13, No. 3/4, 1991). *"A welcome addition to the sparse literature on strategic planning in university libraries. Academic librarians considering strategic planning for their libraries will learn a great deal from this work." (Canadian Library Journal)*

Personnel Administration in an Automated Environment, edited by Philip E. Leinbach, MLS (Vol. 13, No. 1/2, 1990). *"An interesting and worthwhile volume, recommended to university library administrators and to others interested in thought-provoking discussion of the personnel implications of automation." (Canadian Library Journal)*

Library Development: A Future Imperative, edited by Dwight F. Burlingame, PhD (Vol. 12, No. 4, 1990). *"This volume provides an excellent overview of fundraising with special application to libraries. . . . A useful book that is highly recommended for all libraries." (Library Journal)*

Library Material Costs and Access to Information, edited by Sul H. Lee (Vol. 12, No. 3, 1991). *"A cohesive treatment of the issue. Although the book's contributors possess a research library perspective, the data and the ideas presented are of interest and benefit to the entire profession, especially academic librarians." (Library Resources and Technical Services)*

Training Issues and Strategies in Libraries, edited by Paul M. Gherman, MALS, and Frances O. Painter, MLS, MBA (Vol. 12, No. 2, 1990). *"There are . . . useful chapters, all by different authors, each with a preliminary summary of the content–a device that saves much time in deciding whether to read the whole chapter or merely skim through it. Many of the chapters are essentially practical without too much emphasis on theory. This book is a good investment." (Library Association Record)*

Library Education and Employer Expectations, edited by E. Dale Cluff, PhD, MLS (Vol. 11, No. 3/4, 1990). *"Useful to library-school students and faculty interested in employment problems and employer perspectives. Librarians concerned with recruitment practices will also be interested." (Information Technology and Libraries)*

Managing Public Libraries in the 21st Century, edited by Pat Woodrum, MLS (Vol. 11, No. 1/2, 1989). *"A broad-based collection of topics that explores the management problems and possibilities public libraries will be facing in the 21st century." (Robert Swisher, PhD, Director, School of Library and Information Studies, University of Oklahoma)*

Human Resources Management in Libraries, edited by Gisela M. Webb, MLS, MPA (Vol. 10, No. 4, 1989). *"Thought provoking and enjoyable reading. . . . Provides valuable insights for the effective information manager." (Special Libraries)*

Creativity, Innovation, and Entrepreneurship in Libraries, edited by Donald E. Riggs, EdD, MLS (Vol. 10, No. 2/3, 1989). *"The volume is well worth reading as a whole. . . . There is very little repetition, and it should stimulate thought." (Australian Library Review)*

The Impact of Rising Costs of Serials and Monographs on Library Services and Programs, edited by Sul H. Lee (Vol. 10, No. 1, 1989). *". . . Sul Lee hit a winner here." (Serials Review)*

Computing, Electronic Publishing, and Information Technology: Their Impact on Academic Libraries, edited by Robin N. Downes (Vol. 9, No. 4, 1989). *"For a relatively short and easily digestible discussion of these issues, this book can be recommended, not only to those in academic libraries, but also to those in similar types of library or information unit, and to academics and educators in the field." (Journal of Documentation)*

Library Management and Technical Services: The Changing Role of Technical Services in Library Organizations, edited by Jennifer Cargill, MSLS, MSEd (Vol. 9, No. 1, 1988). *"As a practical and instructive guide to issues such as automation, personnel matters, education, management techniques and liaison with other services, senior library managers with a sincere interest in evaluating the role of their technical services should find this a timely publication." (Library Association Record)*

Management Issues in the Networking Environment, edited by Edward R. Johnson, PhD (Vol. 8, No. 3/4, 1989). *"Particularly useful for librarians/information specialists contemplating establishing a local network." (Australian Library Review)*

Acquisitions, Budgets, and Material Costs: Issues and Approaches, edited by Sul H. Lee (Supp. #2, 1988). *"The advice of these library practitioners is sensible and their insights illuminating for librarians in academic libraries." (American Reference Books Annual)*

Pricing and Costs of Monographs and Serials: National and International Issues, edited by Sul H. Lee (Supp. #1, 1987). *"Eminently readable. There is a good balance of chapters on serials and monographs and the perspective of suppliers, publishers, and library practitioners are presented. A book well worth reading." (Australasian College Libraries)*

Legal Issues for Library and Information Managers, edited by William Z. Nasri, JD, PhD (Vol. 7, No. 4, 1987). *"Useful to any librarian looking for protection or wondering where responsibilities end and liabilities begin. Recommended." (Academic Library Book Review)*

Archives and Library Administration: Divergent Traditions and Common Concerns, edited by Lawrence J. McCrank, PhD, MLS (Vol. 7, No. 2/3, 1986). *"A forward-looking view of archives and libraries. . . . Recommend[ed] to students, teachers, and practitioners alike of archival and library science. It is readable, thought-provoking, and provides a summary of the major areas of divergence and convergence." (Association of Canadian Map Libraries and Archives)*

Excellence in Library Management, edited by Charlotte Georgi, MLS, and Robert Bellanti, MLS, MBA (Vol. 6, No. 3, 1985). *"Most beneficial for library administrators . . . for anyone interested in either library/information science or management." (Special Libraries)*

Marketing and the Library, edited by Gary T. Ford (Vol. 4, No. 4, 1984). *Discover the latest methods for more effective information dissemination and learn to develop successful programs for specific target areas.*

Finance Planning for Libraries, edited by Murray S. Martin (Vol. 3, No. 3/4, 1983). *Stresses the need for libraries to weed out expenditures which do not contribute to their basic role–the collection and organization of information–when planning where and when to spend money.*

Planning for Library Services: A Guide to Utilizing Planning Methods for Library Management, edited by Charles R. McClure, PhD (Vol. 2, No. 3/4, 1982). *"Should be read by anyone who is involved in planning processes of libraries–certainly by every administrator of a library or system." (American Reference Books Annual)*

BOOK ORDER FORM!

Order a copy of this book with this form or online at:
http://www.haworthpress.com/store/product.asp?sku=5164

The Changing Landscape for Electronic Resources
Content, Access, Delivery, and Legal Issues

____ in softbound at $29.95 (ISBN: 0-7890-2441-1)
____ in hardbound at $49.95 (ISBN: 0-7890-2440-3)

COST OF BOOKS _____

POSTAGE & HANDLING _____
US: $4.00 for first book & $1.50
for each additional book
Outside US: $5.00 for first book
& $2.00 for each additional book.

SUBTOTAL _____
In Canada: add 7% GST. _____

STATE TAX _____
CA, IL, IN, MN, NY, OH & SD residents
please add appropriate local sales tax.

FINAL TOTAL _____
If paying in Canadian funds, convert
using the current exchange rate,
UNESCO coupons welcome.

❏ BILL ME LATER:
Bill-me option is good on US/Canada/
Mexico orders only; not good to jobbers,
wholesalers, or subscription agencies.

❏ Signature _____

❏ Payment Enclosed: $ _____

❏ PLEASE CHARGE TO MY CREDIT CARD:
❏ Visa ❏ MasterCard ❏ AmEx ❏ Discover
❏ Diner's Club ❏ Eurocard ❏ JCB
Account # _____

Exp Date _____

Signature _____
(Prices in US dollars and subject to change without notice.)

PLEASE PRINT ALL INFORMATION OR ATTACH YOUR BUSINESS CARD

Name

Address

City   State/Province   Zip/Postal Code

Country

Tel   Fax

E-Mail

May we use your e-mail address for confirmations and other types of information? ❏ Yes ❏ No We appreciate receiving
your e-mail address. Haworth would like to e-mail special discount offers to you, as a preferred customer.
We will never share, rent, or exchange your e-mail address. We regard such actions as an invasion of your privacy.

Order From Your **Local Bookstore** or Directly From
The Haworth Press, Inc. 10 Alice Street, Binghamton, New York 13904-1580 • USA
Call Our toll-free number (1-800-429-6784) / Outside US/Canada: (607) 722-5857
Fax: 1-800-895-0582 / Outside US/Canada: (607) 771-0012
E-mail your order to us: orders@haworthpress.com

For orders outside US and Canada, you may wish to order through your local
sales representative, distributor, or bookseller.
For information, see http://haworthpress.com/distributors

(Discounts are available for individual orders in US and Canada only, not booksellers/distributors.)

Please photocopy this form for your personal use.
www.HaworthPress.com

BOF04